YOUR DAUGHTERS SHALL PROPHESY

Women in Ministry in the Church

Edited by

John E. Toews
Valerie Rempel
Katie Funk Wiebe

Winnipeg, MB CANADA   Hillsboro, KS U.S.A.

Your Daughters Shall Prophesy
Copyright © 1992 by Kindred Press, Winnipeg, Manitoba

Published simultaneously by Kindred Press, Winnipeg, Manitoba R2L 1E5 and Kindred Press, Hillsboro, Kansas, 67063.

Canadian Cataloging in Publication Data

Main entry under title:
Your daughters shall prophesy

ISBN: 0-921788-14-2

1. Women clergy - Biblical teaching. 2. Women in church work - Mennonite Brethren Church 3. Women in the Mennonite Brethren Church. 4. Mennonite Brethren Church - Clergy. I. Toews, John E. II. Rempel, Valerie. III. Wiebe, Katie Funk.

BV676.Y88   1992   262'.14973   C92-098034-1

Book design by Lordell Consultants
Cover design by Fred Koop

Printed in Canada by Christian Press

International Standard Book Number 0-921788-14-2

"AND IT SHALL COME TO PASS
IN THE LAST DAYS SAITH GOD,
I WILL POUR OUT OF MY SPIRIT UPON ALL FLESH:
AND YOUR SONS AND
YOUR DAUGHTERS SHALL PROPHESY,
AND YOUR YOUNG MEN SHALL SEE VISIONS,
AND YOUR OLD MEN SHALL DREAM DREAMS:
AND ON MY SERVANTS
AND ON MY HANDMAIDENS
I WILL POUR OUT IN THOSE DAYS OF MY SPIRIT;
AND THEY SHALL PROPHESY."

Acts 2:17-18

i

APPRECIATION

A book is always the product of many persons. In this case the many persons include the Board of Reference and Counsel of the General Conference of Mennonite Brethren Churches which mandated the book; the Reference and Counsel Task Force on Women in Ministry which refined the proposal for the book; the contributors who gracefully accepted numerous editorial suggestions and changes by the editors, as well as delays in publication; Gilbert Brandt, the former editor of Kindred Press who offered valuable editorial assistance; and hundreds of men and women who have asked about the book and encouraged work on it. To the many who have contributed to this book we express our appreciation.

The translation of the Bible used most often in this book is the New International Version (NIV).

John E. Toews
Valerie Rempel
Katie Funk Wiebe

TABLE OF CONTENTS

PREFACE

It is a privilege to offer some reflections and observations on the book you hold in your hands. It is the product of much work on the part of many people. The creation of *Your Daughters Shall Prophesy* was recommended to the Board of Reference and Counsel of the General Conference of Mennonite Brethren Churches by the Task Force on Women in Ministry. The 1987 General Conference convention in Abbotsford, B.C., approved that recommendation, recognizing the need to study this very important issue in our churches.

Conference leadership has been keenly aware of the dimensions of the women's ministry issue for over a decade. While the context of this discussion is much larger than our denomination, it was felt that our churches would benefit from engaging in this dialogue, since our conference resolutions on the role of women (1981 and 1984) surfaced such diverse viewpoints within our ranks.

Thus we offer this book. Its purpose is to study the key biblical passages regarding women in ministry, and it is intended to stimulate study and discussion at the local church level. The reader will notice two different points of view outlined in the book. I wish to remind us that the writers are brothers and sisters of a common faith and good will. They arrive at different understandings of what the Scriptures teach following honest and prayerful study. As noted in the thirteenth chapter of this book, men and women who are deeply committed to Christ can and do interpret God's Word differently. When that happens we must be gracious in our pronouncements (as these writers are) and humbly ac-

vi

knowledge with the Apostle Paul that we still "see through a glass darkly." We ask you to participate in that spirit as well.

As moderator of the General Conference, I invite you to read, reflect, pray, and discuss together with fellow believers in your community of faith. Hopefully the Lord of the church can use these pages to lead us deeper into our understanding of the issues involving women in ministry so that we can find the Spirit's direction and blessing. May we agree that we want to be and do what God wants us to be and do.

Thank you, editors, John E. Toews, Valerie Rempel, and Katie Funk Wiebe, for making this study guide possible. And to all who have written chapters that will help us grow in our understanding, we express our sincere appreciation.

Edmund Janzen
Moderator
Mennonite Brethren Church

HOW TO USE THIS BOOK

Home Bible study groups. Church Bible study groups. Prayer groups. Sunday school classes. Church councils. Leadership groups or retreats. The name doesn't matter. What is important is that you and some other Christians want to study the Bible. You want to learn more about the Scriptures and how to make the truths of the Word work in daily life. You see a small group as an opportunity for the church to come alive.

No two small groups fit the same pattern, but if they are to survive successfully, they usually possess the characteristics given in the following paragraphs.

THE GROUP

Keep the group small enough for personal interaction, yet large enough for meaningful discussion. About twelve to fifteen members who meet regularly is a good size. Plan to have meetings stop and start regularly, and then stick to your schedule.

LEADER

Choose someone to direct the study; call the person a facilitator if you wish. It need not be someone who is an expert in the topic. A facilitator arranges for meeting times, discussion leaders, and so forth without being pushy. Involve both men and women in planning the study and carrying it out.

A SENSE OF PURPOSE

You have begun an interesting and challenging study of a significant topic: the ministry of women in the church. In the process you will learn something about biblical interpretation, about specific scriptural texts, about the way the church functions as an interpreting community of believers, about change, and possibly also about yourself.

COMMITMENT

The group must be committed to regular attendance even when the discussion becomes uncomfortable. Be open to the working of the Holy Spirit. In a small group the Spirit can work if each member is honest about him or herself, is concerned about others and their needs, and is willing to respect confidences. Deny yourself the urge to pry into the inner lives of other members to satisfy your curiosity.

SUFFICIENT STRUCTURE TO ACCOMPLISH THE PURPOSE OF THE GROUP

The Major Issues

Encourage everyone to read pp. 191-198 of Chapter 13 before reading the rest of the book. These pages summarize the major issues in the book, and the issues on which the writers will disagree.

Central Theme

The main point of each chapter is summarized in the Table of Contents. Don't wander from this main point to other side issues even though they may look interesting. Keep track of them and work with them another time.

Bible Study

Read the suggested Scripture passages before coming together. Ask yourself what they say to you. What did the biblical writer intend for them to say to the persons for whom they were originally written? Use more than one translation as you work with the Scripture. Include other materials on the topic, if you desire. Make sure members are clear about the terminology used in each chapter. The writers have tried to keep the language at a layperson's level, but they may not always have succeeded. If needed, slow down and clarify terms and concepts.

Discussion

Ask everyone to formulate a question. Use the questions at the back of the book as a guide to stimulate discussion.

Most people don't like discussion groups if one person monopolizes all the time, if one or more press opinions without any basis for their comments, or if no one feels free to add fresh input or is willing to see other sides of the issue. Don't confuse dead silence with listening silence.

Ask everyone to contribute an answer and to participate even if it is only by looking interested or nodding his or her head. Avoid dropping a matter with "Well, we can pray about it," or "We won't be able to reconcile the matter, so let's go on."

Project for the Week

Encourage each member to pick a project for the week related to the theme to keep it alive in their thoughts until you come together again. This project can be something like asking friends how they deal with the issues under discussion in their family life, listening to a woman preach, teach, or lead the singing, talking to a woman missionary about her role overseas, or discussing with your pastor how he feels about sharing ministry opportunities with women.

Plan to learn more about this important topic so that the pain often associated with it can lead to growth and harmony. The goal is working toward congregational consensus on the issue.

WHY THIS BOOK?

John E. Toews

The Search for Understanding in the Church

Dr. Paul Brand, medical missionary to the lepers of India, often told his audiences that a leprosy patient lacks skin sensation and "nobody realizes what it means when you can't feel pain. You need to surround yourself with new defenses." In Indian villages the rats soon learned that it was quite safe to take a bite from insensitive hands or feet when a person was asleep, so the missionaries provided the patients with cats. "If a person doesn't feel his hand or foot when it is injured, we speak of the foot or hand as dead. It's the pain that makes us realize that the hand or foot belongs to us," said Brand. "Our survival depends upon pain." — Ten Figures for God by Dorothy Clarke Wilson

Pain in the church and a search for understanding is the reason for this book. The church is a particular one, the Mennonite Brethren, a member of the larger family of Anabaptist-Mennonite churches. The search and pain is a universal story. It is the story of people struggling to understand the role and ministry of women in the church, and often of women struggling with the church's resistance to their calling to and giftedness for ministry.

Search

The current Mennonite Brethren search began in 1973. Allen Guenther and Herb Swartz, graduate students in biblical studies in Toronto and faculty members at the Mennonite Brethren Bible College in Winnipeg (now Concord College), wrote an article for the Mennonite Brethren Herald, the publication of the Canadian Mennonite Brethren churches. They argued for the equality of women and men as believers. The Holy Spirit gifts all Christians to lead and to teach, they wrote; the restrictive Pauline texts deal with problems of decorum rather than issues of office. They concluded that women should be encouraged to exercise their gifts in the church.

Twice prior to 1973, the Mennonite Brethren Church had spoken to the issue of women in the church. In 1879 women were allowed to attend conference sessions "as the Spirit leads," as long as they did not teach and remained silent during "the brotherly deliberations." Each local church was freed to decide if women could vote in church meetings.

In 1957, following the ordination of at least 85 women for missionary service over a period of six decades (35 of whom were single), the church determined to differentiate "the public gospel preaching ministry" of men and women by commissioning rather than ordaining women. The intent was not to exclude women from ministry but not to "admit sisters to the public gospel preaching ministry on par with brethren" (General Conference Year Book [GCYB hereafter], 1957, p. 106).

Between 1957 and 1973 a small group of women began to write about their struggle with the church's recent restrictive interpretation. They confessed their pain at the church's refusal to recognize their call to ministry and to affirm their spiritual giftedness. I recall vividly a rather restrictive sermon on 1 Corinthians 14 in a Mennonite Brethren church in early 1973. At least five women spoke with me following the service, several in tears, asking that I speak at the next women's meeting to outline a different understanding of the text. They respected their pastor, but knew in their hearts that there was something wrong with his interpretation of the New Testament. I declined their request because I did not want to become a divisive force in the church.

Six months later I did outline a more affirmative interpretation of the New Testament in a different context halfway across the continent. During the meeting a married woman broke down and cried, almost uncontrollably. After the session she attacked me verbally. She was fearful of the freedom I was offering her in the church. She recoiled in anger despite encouragement from her husband to be more open to the exercise of her gifts in the church. Several years later she found freedom to move into areas of ministry.

The Guenther and Swartz article put the issue on the table for discussion in the church. David Ewert, the leading New Testament teacher in the church, was asked to present a study conference paper to the Canadian Conference in 1974. A modified version of this paper was presented again to a General Conference Study Conference in 1980 (Chapter 2). Ewert affirmed the Guenther and Swartz interpretation. Not only did he acknowledge the complexity of the issue, but he warned the church that it always tends to read the Bible in the light of its own practices. The church is tempted, he observed, to accuse scholars of unfaithfulness when they question such teaching and practice. Ewert exhorted the church not to "absolutize prohibitions" designed to address local first-century excesses. He urged the church to free women for the exercise of their gifts. The only restriction he placed on the ministry of women was the ordained pastoral ministry.

The 1974 Study Conference paper was followed by a Canadian Conference resolution in 1975. It instructed the church to "rethink its traditional stand with respect to the place of the woman in the church. . . . The biblical texts which put strictures on the place of the woman in the Church we believe must be understood, in part, in the context of local violations of the rules of propriety, and in the light of the status of womanhood in the first-century culture" (CCYB, 1975, p. 9). Churches were exhorted to elect women to church committees and councils, and as delegates to church-wide conferences. At the same time, the churches were urged to recognize a distinction between the function of men and women in the church. Women were not to be ordained for the preaching and pastoral ministry nor elected to boards and offices with "eldership" responsibilities.

The 1980 Study Conference paper also resulted in a resolution, this time to the churches of North America through the 1981 General Conference of Mennonite Brethren Churches. The resolution was presented by the Board of Reference and Counsel (BORAC). It encouraged the churches to discover and utilize the spiritual resources of women for "various ministries in the church and in the world" including "participation in local

church and conference ministries" (GCYB, 1981, p. 47).
Such ministry was limited only by the final clause that
"the Mennonite Brethren should not ordain women to
pastoral leadership." The resolution was meant "to encourage the expanded involvement of women in the
work of the church, not to limit their ministry." But the
delegates perceived the resolution as restrictive.
Therefore, they received it with the understanding that
it be edited to read more positively.

BORAC reported to the next General Conference in
1984 that the question of "the ministry of women in our
churches" remained an unsettled issue and needed continued study. It recognized that an increasing number of
women were graduating with seminary degrees, and encouraged "the churches and our conferences to be open
to their services." The board asserted that "more encouragement and more open doors for service should be giv-
en to our sisters." It also reported that it intended to ex-
pand the 1981 resolution for the next convention.

BORAC presented its more affirmative and expanded resolution to the General Conference in 1987.
The resolution read as follows:

> We believe that God created both men and women in his
> image, and therefore both share an equal humanity before
> God (Gen. 1:27).

> We believe that all Christians are joint heirs with Christ,
> and therefore both women and men experience full salva-
> tion in him (Gal. 3:28).

> We believe that the Spirit grants gifts to all believers, ir-
> respective of gender, for diverse ministries both in the
> church and in the world, and therefore both men and
> women minister God's grace (1 Pet. 4:10).

We believe that God calls all women and men to serve in the church and in the world; we also believe he calls some women, as well as some men, for ministries within the context of the church (Acts 2:17, 18; Eph. 4:1ff.; Rom. 12:4-8; 1 Pet. 4:10).

We believe that since God has gifted and called both men and women, the church should recognize and affirm them in their ministry for the common good of the church (1 Cor. 12:7; Rom. 16:1-16).

We urge that the Mennonite Brethren churches free and affirm women for ministries in the church, at home and abroad, e.g., decision-making (committees and boards), evangelizing (visitation and discipling), teaching (Bible study and preaching), pastoral counseling (shepherding and soul care). We affirm women as associate pastors or "leading elders." (We recognize that the ordination of women in ministry is an issue that is not addressed in this statement. It is not addressed because ordination is an issue in the Mennonite Brethren Church for many men as well as women. Therefore BORAC will address the question of ordination in the future).

We acknowledge that the evangelical church, worldwide, is in transition in its understanding of the scope of ministries of women in the church and world. Many evangelicals believe that neither 1 Cor. 14:34, 35 nor 1 Tim. 2:11-15 "rules out the ordination of women as preachers, teachers or leaders in the church" (Christianity Today, October 3, 1986). Other evangelicals believe these texts are more restrictive. Mennonite Brethren people also differ in their interpretation of these texts. We recognize that significant exegetical issues are involved in these alternatives. Therefore BORAC recommends a careful biblical study process by our congregations on the role and ministry of women in the church, and has commissioned the preparation of a book and study guide of all relevant biblical passages.

The resolution was historic. It affirmed the full humanity, salvation, giftedness and calling of women to ministry. The implications were debated. The points at issue were the reference to preaching, the affirmation of the associate pastoral role, and the positive reference to ordination by <u>Christianity Today.</u> The resolution was approved with the following revision of the last two paragraphs:

> We encourage our churches to free and affirm women for ministries in the church, at home and abroad, in decision-making, evangelizing, teaching, counseling, encouragement, music, youth, visitations, etc.
>
> BORAC recommends a careful biblical study process by our congregations on the role and ministry of women in the church, and has commissioned the preparation of a book and study guide of all relevant biblical passages.

This book is the result of the BORAC mandate. It is a function of a search for better understanding of the role and ministry of women in the church.

Between the 1987 Conference resolution and the publication of this book, the Mennonite Brethren Church studied the issue in another study conference held at Normal, Illinois, in 1989. Tim Geddert, a seminary professor, argued that the conference should affirm diversity by freeing individual churches to shape their own exegetical conclusions and practices. Ed Boschman, a pastor, made the case for a return to the pre-1981 stance of no women in public church leadership [see <u>Direction,</u> 18 (1989)].

As illustrated above, the search for understanding is characterized by disagreement. The point of the disagreement is the interpretation of the Bible, specifically the so-called "restrictive" texts. Since 1973 the Bible teachers at the Mennonite Brethren Bible College (Winnipeg) and the Mennonite Brethren Biblical

Seminary (Fresno) have consistently offered affirmative interpretations of the biblical teachings as a whole and of the "restrictive" texts in particular (see Guenther and Swartz in 1973, David Ewert in 1974 and 1980, Howard Loewen in 1977, John E. Toews in 1980 and 1988, George Konrad in 1982). But in many local churches and in conference discussions a significant number of pastors have insisted on traditional interpretations (see the Boschman article as a typical case study). The teachers and pastors in the church disagree. Many lay people are confused; some are getting angry at the divisiveness such disagreement among church leaders sows in the church.

Pain

The church is searching for new and clearer understanding because many women are crying out for healing from the pain of rejection and exclusion from ministry. They are profoundly aware of their spiritual giftedness. They report clear calls to church ministry. They hear a "yes" from God, but a "no" from the church. The contradiction between their experience with God and their experience in the church is intense. More and more women are speaking of their pain and anger. Five stories told in Mennonite Brethren churches illustrate the pain.

A few years ago I visited with a young woman from a prominent Mennonite Brethren family. She graduated *magna cum laude* from one of the most prestigious universities in North America. Her parents and some friends in the church were encouraging her to consider the ministry. When I asked her how she was responding to this encouragement, she told me that it was not an option for her because of the church's stance on women in ministry. "I can go anywhere I want in the world," she replied, "and I will not wait for the church to catch up on this issue."

Another very intelligent young Mennonite Brethren woman requested an appointment with me. She wanted to talk about the proposition "that she could not be a Christian and a woman." When I asked her to explain, she argued on the basis of 1 Timothy 2 that a woman cannot really be saved. If women are excluded from the ministry, she asserted, because of Eve's participation in the fall, but men are not despite Adam's participation in the fall, what that really means is that men can be fully saved but women cannot. And if she could not be fully saved because she was a woman, then she did not want to be a Christian. "To be a Christian and a woman" is contradictory, she said over and over again. She found nothing I said reassuring.

Another woman was converted at mid-life from paganism. Sometime thereafter she heard "a still small voice" calling her to the ministry. She resisted for several years because she knew the stance of the church. The sense of call persisted and after much struggle she yielded. She experienced a profound peace in her life. She completed seminary and serves in a church. Her church affirms her gifts for ministry, but she continues to struggle. "It is not an easy choice for a woman to make," she said with a great deal of pain, "because it means going against the expectation of women."

A young woman was converted through the ministry of a new, urban Mennonite Brethren church. She grew rapidly in the faith. Her local church began to affirm her gifts and leadership. She felt a call to the ministry. With the support of her church she entered seminary to train for church ministry. She became aware for the first time in seminary that her call to ministry was a problem in the church. Suddenly she struggled because her call and local church affirmation were out of step with the larger church.

Another young woman grew up in a Mennonite Brethren minister's home. Over time she became very much involved in the church and in her father's ministry. She had no sense from her father or the church that her involvement in ministry was a problem. In fact, she experienced special support and affirmation from the older people in the church. As an adult she sensed a call to full-time church ministry. She entered seminary, and graduated. But now she was a problem. She could not find a place of ministry.

There are women in the church who live with enormous, often unbearable pain because the church says "no" to their gifts and calling from God. Some of these women deal with the pain by leaving the church. Others faithfully serve wherever they can while praying and hoping for a clearer affirmation from the church. Still others are training for the ministry to which they have been called in the hope that the church will soon open its doors to their desire and calling to serve.

These women are our daughters. We have birthed and nurtured them in our families and our churches. They are our daughters whom God has called to prophesy (Acts 2:17). They wonder if we will let them answer the call of God. They cry in our homes and in our churches because they hear more **no's** than **yes's**. They also continue to live in hope that the biblical prophecy, "your daughters will prophesy," will become a reality for them.

But other women also feel pain. Women who have chosen to stay home to raise their families, who have chosen to work in traditional types of ministry such as local women's missionary groups, Sunday school teaching, relief sewing, and similar activities, often feel slapped in the face by the clamor for women's greater involvement in church ministries. Have their many years of long and submissive service, joyfully given, been worth nothing? They feel fulfilled. They have no desire for anything more. They are using their gifts as they believe God wants them to, but now they feel pushed into second-best status in God's kingdom. They also want an end to their confusion.

Women are not the only ones suffering in the church. When one member suffers, all suffer. I visited with a father recently whose daughter has left the church because of the church's stance on women in ministry. His pain is profound, his confusion without bounds. Why does the church say "no" to his daughter? Why can his daughter not be more patient with the church? Tears rolled down his cheeks as we talked.

Husbands feel hurt by accusations that they aren't allowing their wives to achieve a fulfilled life. They and their wives feel pressured to accept interpretations of Scripture alien to their view of life. They also know pain.

A veteran church leader spoke to me recently about his confusion. There was a time when he was clear on the issue of women in ministry, he reported. But within the last several months he had visited with several women who spoke of their call to ministry. "Their call is as clear as mine," he confided. "How can I say no to their call? I am beginning to change my mind." And then he added, "In ten years we will accept women into the ministry. If it will be okay in ten years, I want to know why it is not all right today?"

During a visit with a pastor friend a few years ago the question of women in ministry came up. He was very troubled by any attempt to read the restrictive texts as first-century and culture specific or to limit the meaning of the texts, e.g., 1 Corinthians 14, to not asking questions, or 1 Timothy 2, to learning properly or to unlearned women. I pulled my Greek New Testament out of my briefcase and translated the texts very literally and carefully, trying to show him an alternative way to understand these texts. Suddenly, in considerable exasperation, he said, "That is not what my Bible says. It says 'women should keep silent' and 'women should not teach or have authority over men.'" Any other reading was due to liberalism and secular feminism, he proclaimed. Even though we had been friends for many years, he expressed real fear, even anger, that I was becoming a theological liberal. Nothing I could say would persuade him that I was still solidly evangelical. Our trust relationship had been fractured. Relationship is strained because we read the same Bible and the same specific texts to say different things.

The pain women experience in the church is increased by the discrepancy between words and actions. Since 1974, conference resolutions have exhorted the churches and conferences to affirm women for church and conference ministries, but women experience more resistance and hostility than affirmation. In 1984, women represented only 8.6% of the membership of General Conference boards, compared to 32.5% in the General Conference of Mennonites and 35.6% in the Mennonite Church. The 1984 resolution specifically encouraged churches to utilize seminary-trained women in ministry. An increasing number of women are graduating from seminaries, but few find openness to ministry in the church.

The Intent of This Book

The intent of this book is to stimulate Bible study and discussion in local churches about the role of women in church ministry. The book was mandated by BORAC to address these issues. BORAC asked John E. Toews, a member of the board, Valerie Rempel and Katie Funk Wiebe to edit a book that would call upon a group of teachers in the church, both men and women, to study the critical biblical texts involved in the discussion of women in church ministry. BORAC reviewed a draft of the book in 1989, and recommended some significant changes. It reviewed the final draft in 1990 and recommended its publication as a study guide in the churches.

The book is primarily a Bible study. Nine of the thirteen chapters study biblical texts.

The focus is Bible study because the issue in the church is defined as one of biblical interpretation. Mennonite Brethren, with other evangelicals, believe the Bible is the sole and ultimate authority for questions of belief and practice. A former consensus about how to interpret the Bible has broken down. Alternative interpretations exist. The struggle in the church is over how to understand the Bible correctly in the midst of changes in society and in the context of diverse interpretations of biblical texts.

The book begins with two general studies. The first is a shortened version of David Ewert's 1980 Study Conference paper. The second study, written by Elmer Martens, makes the case for a permanent "creation order" that frees women for ministry within the context of overall male leadership.

The other eight biblical chapters study the specific texts central to the discussion in the church. Two chap-

ters on Old Testament texts suggest a stronger emphasis on equality than Martens sees. The New Testament
studies consistently affirm women for ministry among
the people of God. The restrictive texts are reviewed
with special care, and fresh interpretations are proposed
that will need to be tested in the church. All writers affirm the general direction of Ewert's paper, and cau-
tiously challenge the significance of the creation order in
the New Testament.

The clear message of the book is that one can accept
the full authority of the Bible and read it carefully and
seriously as affirming women for ministry in the church
either within the context of overall male leadership or
independent of male leadership. That message will pro-
voke more discussion, perhaps even disagreement, in
the church. It is presented by the editors and writers
with the hope and the prayer that the church's understanding of the Bible will be deepened and enlarged
through study and that all the gifts of the Spirit will be
freed for ministry in the body of Christ.

Alternative interpretations are identified in the
book. The most accessible of these interpretations are
listed below.

MAJOR MENNONITE BRETHREN WRITINGS

Boschman, Ed. "Women's Role in Ministry in the Church."
    Direction 18 (1989): 44-53.

Ewert, David. "The Christian Woman in the Church and
    Conference." Yearbook of the Canadian Conference of
    Mennonite Brethren Churches, 63rd Convention, July 6-9,
    1974: 30-43.

_____. "The Place of Woman in the Church." Unpublished Paper, Board of Reference and Counsel Study Conference, Clearbrook, B.C., 1980.

Geddert, Timothy. "The Ministry of Women: A Proposal for Mennonite Brethren." Direction 18 (1989): 54-71.

Guenther, Allen, and Herb Swartz. "The Role of Women in the Church." Mennonite Brethren Herald 12 (4 May 1973): 4-9.

Konrad, George. "In the Image of God." Christian Leader 45 (2 November 1982): 6-9.

_____. "Joint Heirs in Christ." Christian Leader 45 (16 November 1982): 5-7.

_____. "Partners in Ministry." Christian Leader 45 (30 November 1982): 2-4.

Loewen, Howard. "The Pauline View of Woman." Direction 6 (October 1977): 3-20.

Swartz, Herb. "Women and the Church." The Bible and the Church. Essays in Honour of David Ewert, ed. A.J. Dueck, H.J. Giesbrecht, V.G. Shillington. Kindred Press, 1988. 95-110.

Toews, John E. "The Role of Women in the Church: The Pauline Perspective." Direction 9 (January 1980): 25-35.

_____. "Women in Church Leadership." The Bible and the Church. Essays in Honour of David Ewert, ed. A.J. Dueck, H.J. Giesbrecht, V.G. Shillington. Kindred Press, 1988. 75-93.

MAJOR EVANGELICAL LITERATURE

Bilezikian, Gilbert. Beyond Sex Roles. Baker, 1985.

Clark, Stephen B. Man and Woman in Christ. Servant Books, 1980.

Evans, Mary J. Woman in the Bible. InterVarsity, 1983.

Foh, Susan. Women and the Word of God. Baker, 1979.

Hurley, James B. Man and Woman in Biblical Perspective. Zondervan, 1981.

Michelson, Alvera, ed. Women, Authority and the Bible. InterVarsity, 1986.

Piper, John and Wayne Gruden, eds., Recovering Biblical Manhood and Womanhood. Crossway Books, 1991.

Swartley, Willard M. Slavery, Sabbath, War and Women. Herald Press, 1983.

MEMBERS BY GRACE [1]   2

David Ewert

They Labored in the Gospel

Disagreements concerning the ministry of women in the church are not resolved by simply affirming the authority of the word of God. It is rather a question of how one interprets the Scriptures.

The question, in this particular case, is complicated by the fact that the apostolic writers seem to move in two directions. There are, on the one hand, those passages which stress the freedom which Christian women have in Christ. On the other hand, we have several passages that seem to put restrictions on the kind of ministry women can perform in the congregation.

I. NEW FREEDOM IN CHRIST

The text that most succinctly expresses the equality of male and female in Christ is Galatians 3:28: "There is

---

1 This chapter is an edited version of the 1980 Board of Reference and Counsel Study Conference paper.

neither Jew nor Greek, slave nor free, male nor female, for you are all one in Christ Jesus." In the context Paul is discussing the condition for full inclusion in the Abrahamic covenant (v. 29). The one condition is justification by faith (expressed in baptism, v. 27).

This passage does not deny sexual differences between male and female any more than it denies ethnic distinctions (Jew and Greek) or socio-economic evils (slave and free). In Christ, however, these distinctions are transcended. There is something strikingly new here, for in earlier times women were members of the covenant by virtue of men; in the church women are members by grace on the basis of faith.

Peter joins Paul in giving Christian women a new place in Christ when he counsels husbands to give their wives honor "as heirs with you of the gracious gift of life" (1 Pet. 3:7). Whereas the physical differences remain, spiritually a woman shares equally with her husband in the grace of God and in his gift of eternal life.

Women were the first witnesses of the resurrection (Mk. 16:1-8). They were among the 120 who experienced the coming of the Spirit and the birth of the church (Acts 1:14). There were many converts from among women in Jerusalem (Acts 5:14), in Samaria (Acts 8:12), and in the Gentile world. Mary, the mother of Mark, put her house at the disposal of the early church (Acts 12:12).

When Paul and his associates brought the gospel to Europe, it began with the conversion of Lydia (Acts 16:13ff.). Her household became a base for further operations. At Thessalonica a great many "leading women" became charter members of the church (Acts 17:4). Luke notes that an Athenian woman heard Paul's Areopagus address and believed the Gospel. Evidently she was an outstanding woman, for she is mentioned by name (Damaris, Acts 17:34).

In Corinth Paul encountered a Jewish couple, Priscilla and Aquila, who became his coworkers in the Gospel (Acts 18:3). When Paul left for Syria, the couple went to Ephesus and became the spiritual mentors to Apollos (Acts 18:26). Later this couple moved back to Rome where a church met in their house. Paul greets "Prisca and Aquila, my fellow workers in Christ Jesus," in Romans (16:3, 4) and again in 2 Timothy (4:19). In the six references to this outstanding Christian couple, Priscilla's name stands first four times. Some later scribes caught the significance of this order, and reversed it, for it seemed improper to have Aquila's name after his wife's. Was Priscilla more gifted than her husband? Did she come from a higher social class? We do not know, but it is possible that she took the lead when Apollos was instructed in the faith.

Although it is difficult to define what "prophecy" means in every instance in the New Testament, the evangelist Philip's four daughters had the gift of prophecy (Acts 21:9). Some form of ministry is implied.

No one reading the Book of Acts could come to the conclusion that the early church was led by women. On the other hand, it is also clear that they played a vital role in the life of the church from the beginning. The fact that Paul persecuted not only men but also women (Acts 9:2) shows what a force they were in the expansion of the Christian faith. Paul says explicitly that women helped him in his labors. For example, he mentions Euodia and Syntyche as those who "contended at my side in the cause of the gospel, along with Clement and the rest of my fellow workers..." (Phil. 4:3).

Perhaps nowhere is Paul's appreciation for the work of Christian women seen as clearly as in Romans 16. Of 26 persons mentioned, nine or ten are women. The list starts with Phoebe, who, it seems, was entrusted with the letter to the Romans. She is called *diakonos*, which probably means "deaconess" (this is possibly the meaning in 1 Tim. 3:11 also, i.e., "women-deacons" rather than "wives of deacons"). Paul recommends her to the Roman church as a saint who had helped him and many others (vv. 1, 2). Of Prisca and Aquila he says that these fellow-workers "risked their lives for me" (v. 4), and among the friends whom he greets is Mary (v. 6), "who worked very hard for you" (i.e., the Roman church).

Scholars wish we knew more about Junia (Julia) and Andronicus (v. 7), but it is impossible to decide whether the name Junia (Julia) is feminine or masculine. If feminine then we have a staggering word of praise applied to her: "outstanding among the apostles." (Chrysostom in the fourth century wrote: "Oh! how great is the devotion of this woman, that she should be counted worthy of the appellation of apostle.") Two other women, Tryphaena and Tryphosa (v. 12), are also given honorable mention as "those who work hard in the Lord." Philologus and Julia were possibly a husband-wife team (v. 15). Paul also singles out Nereus and his sister for Christian greeting (v. 15).

There is no doubt that the mission of the early church was greatly strengthened by the contributions of Christian women. The question of how they actually functioned in the Christian assemblies is not as clear. In 1 Corinthians 11:5 women pray and prophesy in public, observing, of course, the rules of propriety in the matter of dress—which in Paul's day meant wearing the customary headcovering.

There are, however, two passages in which Paul seems to limit Christian women in what they may do in the Christian assembly.

II. APPARENT RESTRICTIONS IN MINISTRY

1. 1 Corinthians 14:34-36. "Women should remain silent in the churches. They are not allowed to speak, but must be in submission, as the Law says. If they want to inquire about something, they should ask their own husbands at home; for it is disgraceful for a woman to speak in the church."

Let me mention some ways in which interpreters have tried to harmonize this passage with 1 Corinthians 11, where women are seen as participating both in the mission of the church and in the church's worship.

a. Since this passage appears after verse 40 in some manuscripts and appears to disrupt the flow of Paul's thought on tongues and prophecy, some say this passage is an insertion and is un-Pauline. While that is highly doubtful, that explanation would still not relieve the problem. Even if this passage had come from the pen of another apostolic writer, we would still be faced with the meaning of what is written.

b. Another view is that Chapter 11 has in mind the worship of the church, which was open to outsiders, whereas Chapter 14 describes a membership meeting. Another form of this view is that Chapter 11 describes the worship experience of believers only, at which Christian women had the freedom to pray and prophesy, while 1 Corinthians 14 describes a meeting at which unbelievers might also be present. In such meetings women should be silent to avoid offending others.

c. Another way out of the dilemma is to argue that Paul mentions the praying and prophesying of women (Ch. 11), but does not condone it. However, since he condemns inappropriate attire, one would expect him to censure women for praying and prophesying, if he objected to such activity.

d. "Pray and prophesy" in Chapter 11 means, so it is argued, to participate in worship and to receive all the blessings of worship but not actually that women who participated in worship prayed and prophesied themselves. That, however, seems contrary to Paul's assumption that they did pray and prophesy.

e. Michael Green is of the opinion that the "speaking" which is forbidden in Chapter 14 is speaking in tongues, since the entire chapter deals with that topic (Called to Serve, p. 56).

f. Krister Stendahl holds that "the context (v. 35) makes it clear that the silence here stands in contrast to 'asking questions' not to preaching, teaching or prophesying. That being so, there is no tension between this passage and the clear reference in Chapter 11 to the fact that women may prophesy." Paul forbids disruptive questioning in church and advises women to ask their husbands at home. Perhaps they were questioning the message of Christian prophets, assuming too much authority.

g. Another approach is to see in this passage a failure on Paul's part to bring his practice into line with his theory. However, to accuse Paul of a lapse at this point would get us into serious trouble, for then we could get rid of Paul whenever he did not agree with us, or vice versa. A more sensible approach (if one follows this line of thought) is to recognize that in the first generation Paul could not force the church to break longstanding cultural patterns. Just as he could not overcome slavery in his day (while holding to the freedom of the slave in Christ), so he could not allow woman to go farther than society would allow, if the church was not to come into complete disrepute.

I think it is obvious that Paul did not mean the command for silence to be understood in the absolute sense, otherwise women could not have participated in song, prayer, and confessions of faith. The reminder to be submissive may suggest that some women did not know how to handle their newly-found liberties and were assuming what was generally held to be a man's prerogative, namely, leadership. Paul seems to have the creation account in mind when he counsels submission—"as the Law says"—suggesting that the new order of redemption has not done away with the order of creation. Some scholars take this reference to the law to be an allusion to Genesis 3:16, where the husband's rule over the wife is mentioned. F.F. Bruce, however, thinks it is rather a reference to the creation account. Of course, Genesis 3:16 stands in the context of the curse, and it is somewhat hard to see why Paul would refer to the curse as a binding arrangement.

Paul clearly wants women to be informed on matters of faith. "If they want to inquire about something, they should ask their own husbands at home." We tend to be offended by this stricture, and overlook how revolutionary the passage actually was. Whereas the rabbis thought that to teach women the Torah was like teaching them to sin, Paul wants women to learn.

Leon Morris (in a public lecture) pointed out that in both the restrictive passages (1 Cor. 14 and 1 Tim. 2) Paul mentions the "learning" of women. Implied, Morris suggests, is that, once they have learned, they will also be permitted greater freedom and fuller participation in public worship. It would then be wrong to universalize and to "freeze" the command to silence for all times. By implication, we could say that once she had learned, and once she found herself in a situation where it was not considered improper for a woman to speak in public, she might well be asked to do so.

2. **1 Timothy 2:11-12.** "A woman should learn in quietness and full submission. I do not permit a woman to teach or have authority over a man; she must be silent. For Adam was formed first, then Eve. And Adam was not the one deceived; it was the woman who was deceived and became a sinner."

In a day when women did not teach elsewhere in public, it would have been out of character if Paul had thrown open the doors and encouraged women to become leaders in the church. Moreover, the heretical teachings which Paul combats in this letter may have been furthered by untaught women who had, by virtue of their gifts, taken leadership in teaching. Some interpreters infer from this that once women have learned they may teach, but for the moment Paul wants them to desist.

Learning in quietness probably meant that women should not raise objections to what was taught. Speaking and "silence" are not mutually exclusive. For example, when Peter reported on his fellowship with Gentiles (Acts 11), the Jewish brothers became "quiet" and "praised God." Did they praise God in silence? Hardly! But they did not object to Peter's fellowship with the Gentiles. Or, take Acts 21:14, where the disciples at Caesarea tried to dissuade Paul from going to Jerusalem. When they couldn't, they were "quiet" and "said": "The will of the Lord be done." Clearly, to be quiet does not mean that they said nothing, but rather it means they did not object. This would be in line with 1 Corinthians 14 where constant interruption with questions or even objections would cause confusion in worship.

In 1 Timothy 2 "silence" probably means the opposite of lording it over husbands. Indeed quietness here is linked with submission—the kind that is expected of all church members (Eph. 5:20) and even of male prophets who speak (1 Cor. 14:30). Certainly Paul does not mean that women are not to be heard in church, but rather they are not to wrangle and argue.

Verse 12, however, states clearly that it is inappropriate for a woman to teach or to lord it over a man; she is to be "in quietness," i.e., in submission.

That he did not forbid women to teach altogether is clear: Priscilla taught Apollos (Acts 18:13, 24-26); Euodia and Syntyche labored side by side with Paul in the gospel, and we take that to mean that they did more than prepare food and wash clothes (Phil. 4:2ff.). Paul, of course, wants women to teach their children (2 Tim. 1:5; 3:15)—how, otherwise, would Timothy have known the Scriptures from childhood? Older women are urged to teach younger women (Tit. 2:3-5). If they participated in prayer and prophecy when the church gathered (1 Cor. 11), they exercised some kind of teaching function.

Clearly, then, the prohibition forbidding women to teach is not to be made absolute, for it was not made absolute in New Testament times. Nor have we made it absolute in the twentieth century, for we have never thought it inappropriate for women serving as missionaries to instruct future male pastors of mission churches.

Some see the way out of the dilemma by dis-
tinguishing between two kinds of teaching in the early
church: instruction, exhortation, proclamation (in which
women might participate), and authoritative, dis-
ciplinary, perhaps doctrinal teaching (in which they
should not take part). However, such a distinction is
hard to make on the basis of the New Testament.

Others see the restriction as limited to leadership
functions. Perhaps "to teach" and *authenteo* ("to act out
of oneself" and then to act autocratically, or to interrupt)
are used in parallel fashion here. By implication, a woman may well instruct the congregation, if it is done under the leadership of a man.

Again, others insist on universalizing and "freezing"
this prohibition without taking into account the situation in which these instructions were given. The ascetic
emphasis in Gnosticism, an early Christian heresy
which distinguished body and spirit, may have led to a
disparagement of family life, marriage, and childbirth
on the part of some women who insisted on playing a
leading role in the teaching ministry of the church (perhaps v. 15 suggests that). We may have a situation in
Ephesus such as is reflected in the letter to Thyatira
(Rev. 2:18ff.): "I have this against you: You tolerate the
woman Jezebel, who calls herself a prophetess. By her
teaching she misleads my servants into sexual immoral-
ity and the eating of food sacrificed to idols." This would
be the libertine wing of Gnosticism.

Donald Guthrie suggests that the prohibition may
have been due to the greater facility with which contemporary women were falling under the influence of
impostors. And that may be instructive when we look at
Paul's rationale for the prohibition. "And Adam was not
deceived but the woman was thoroughly deceived and

fell into transgression." Several interpretations have
been suggested. First, we may detect the Gnostic tendency to despise marriage and family in the interest of
greater holiness and openness to God. Paul may be
warning such women that just as Eve, when she was
alone, was approached by the Tempter and fell into sin,
they better watch themselves. That there were such de-
ceivers who forbade marriage can be seen from 1
Timothy 4:3. Another interpretation says that Paul
counsels against giving women positions of authority in
the church because they are by nature more perceptive
and responsive and so in greater danger of being led
astray. A third interpretation is that since Eve tried to
lead once and created chaos for humanity, her punishment for all times is that she may not lead. This is
problematic, if for no other reason than that elsewhere
in the New Testament Adam stands at the head of the
sinful race. Moreover, it would mean that Paul's instructions regarding women in the church were determined not by what has happened in Christ, but by
what has happened in sin. The very next verse reminds
us that women, too, experience Christ's salvation. A
fourth possibility is to say with Paul Jewett that Paul's
argument reflects a leftover of his rabbinic thinking, but
it will hardly do to say that Paul is in error at those
points where we cannot harmonize him with other passages or with current sentiments.

III. TOWARD A POSSIBLE SOLUTION

Should Christian women be restricted in their use of
spiritual gifts? Does the equality of men and women in
Christ refer to spiritual status only or also to function?
How are we to harmonize statements in Paul's writings

that seem to be contradictory? Since Paul's teachings were given in particular historical and cultural situations, are they all equally and permanently binding for every conceivable historical or cultural situation? What happens when the gospel takes root in a matriarchal society? If Paul was concerned about the deportment of women in the congregation in order to insure the reputation of the church in the community, how does the church express this concern today in a society which might interpret the church's traditional stance as a form of repression? What about single women in the church, to whom the texts which speak of the marriage relationship hardly apply directly? Or do they?

These and other questions beg for answers, but the answers are hard to come by. Quoting chapter and verse often means selecting a particular chapter and verse which best expresses our feelings on the matter and either overlooking passages which point in the opposite direction, or subordinating such passages to our preferred texts.

We know that churches are coming to different conclusions on this matter. Some take the restrictive passages to be a kind of "hangover" of Paul's patriarchal mentality and therefore not a word of God for all times. This is, I think, a wrongheaded approach to Scripture. By contrast, some universalize, make absolute the commands of Paul for the silence of women in the congregation. This approach is hard to harmonize with the New Testament as a whole. It overlooks the fact that Paul was seeking to curb excesses and pays no attention to the cultural setting of the New Testament.

Others hold firmly to these passages as a divinely inspired word of God but a word which came in a given cultural form. Once the form changes, the word must be applied in new ways. The danger in this approach is that we not only apply the truth to a different situation but do away with the truth altogether. Then there are those who hold that the restrictive passages are in line with God's creation order in which man's headship is established. Redemption affects the tragic consequences of sin but does not undo the relationship of man and woman established by the Creator. In practice this might express itself in one of several ways: either a woman should not teach at all when men are present; or she may teach as long as a man leads; or she may not teach if she is married but may if she is single; or she may teach but may not assume the pastoral leadership of the church.

It is clear that Christian women share in all the blessings of God's redeeming grace as Christian men do. It would also be difficult to show from Scripture that women are less endowed with gifts of the Spirit (*charismata*) than men. That by itself does not settle the question, of course, because relatively few men exercise their gifts in the worship services of the church. Gifts are given for service, and the services of the church members are largely done in the world. The church gathers only to be strengthened for its services during the week.

It is my understanding that Paul's command for women to be silent in the church's assemblies must be understood, in part, in the light of the status of womanhood in his society. Had the apostle not taken the feelings and prejudices of the contemporary patriarchal world into account, there would have been utter chaos. This means that where cultural patterns differ, Paul's strictures must also be modified. Women no longer wear Near-Eastern kerchiefs to church, and yet presumably they confess to be in harmony with 1 Corinthians 11, since in our society women do not need to have a head-covering to be appropriately dressed.

Slavery was an evil institution, yet Paul did not crusade against it, for to do so would have meant defeat and utter chaos. But that did not mean that he condoned the status quo (as Gal. 3:28 indicates). Similarly, some of the things Paul has to say about women in the church are an accommodation to people's feelings about their status at the time. This does not mean that Paul condoned what Jewish and pagan culture had done to them.   And just as Christianity planted seeds that would lead to the abolition of slavery, so it also restored womanhood to true dignity.

We should be careful, then, not to make absolute prohibitions which were designed to curb excesses in local situations about which we are not sufficiently informed—particularly in light of the fact that there are passages which seem to point in the opposite direction.

It would appear to me, after considering the various options, that we should encourage women to participate actively at the various levels of church, mission, and denominational activity. However, given the fact that the apostles put some restrictions on women, we should leave the leadership of churches in the hands of men who have been equipped by God and are called by the congregation for this ministry.

ADAM NAMED HER EVE

Elmer A. Martens

The Importance of Creation Order

> Adam: "Sole Eve, associate sole, to me beyond
> Compare above all living creatures dear!
> Well hast thou motioned, well thy thoughts employed
> How we might best fulfill the work which here
> God hath assigned us, nor of me shalt pass
> Unpraised; for nothing lovelier can be found
> In a woman than to study household good,
> And good works in her husband to promote.
> Yet not so strictly hath our Lord imposed
> Labor as to debar us when we need
> Refreshment, whether food or talk between,
> Food of the mind, or this sweet intercourse
> Of looks and smiles . . . — John Milton, _Paradise Lost_

The critical issue in the biblical interpretation of women in church ministry is the starting point. Anabaptists give major weight to Jesus and the gospels. The departure point for the discussion about women and men in ministry must be Jesus' practice and teaching. His teaching harked back to the creation order.

Jesus broke with the customs of his day, which regarded women as second-class citizens or worse (Mk. 7:24-30; Jn. 4; Matt. 27:55-56; Lk. 10:38-42; Jn. 20:1-18). It follows that the depreciation of women relatively common in some church and family circles is contrary to the model set by Jesus. Men in leadership have ample reason to apologize to the women in our churches for attitudes and actions not in the spirit of Christ.

Jesus' practice must be balanced with his teaching. A striking feature of that teaching was his stress on the creation pattern as normative. When the opponents query Jesus about divorce, Jesus quickly makes clear that, while he acknowledges the Mosaic teaching on divorce, the intended pattern was set in Eden: one husband, one wife (Matt. 19:1-12). Paul, like Jesus, grounds his position in the creation (1 Cor. 11:8; 1 Tim. 2:13). It is only reasonable then, when seeking light on the question of men, women and ministry, that attention be given to the opening chapters of Genesis.

THE ORDERING AT CREATION

Ordering is a chief concern of Genesis 1—2. The arrangement of the acts of creation in six days presents a carefully laid-out sequence. The celestial bodies of sun and moon were set in place in order to rule over day and night; human beings were to rule over the earth. The great sin reported in Genesis 3 is that human beings were taken in by the tempter who promised them that by eating of the tree human beings could be like God. Eve succumbed to the temptation and trespassed the appointed order.

The first and highly significant statement made about men and women is "and God created man in his own image, in the image of God he created him; male and female he created them" (Gen. 1:27). The initial word is a word about equality. Both women and men are created in God's image. There is no hint here of superiority or inferiority. While the gender distinction is noted, each has identical dignity. Humans are not, as in the ancient Near-East myths, slaves of the gods, but beings who are "a little lower than God" (Ps. 8:5). In whatever way that "image" is to be understood, there is no argument that both women and men share worth and dignity equally.

They share equally also in another respect. God gives both man and woman the command to have dominion over the earth and to rule over it: "And God blessed them; and God said to them, 'Be fruitful and multiply, and fill the earth, and subdue it . . .'" (Gen. 1:28). So Genesis 1 places women equal with men as to position before God, and equal with men in environmental stewardship.

The so-called second creation account (Gen. 2:4b-24) speaks again to the question of environment and also addresses the man/woman relationship. How these two accounts of creation are to be understood has received different answers. One view is that they stem from different sources and have been combined. A more likely view is that the first (1:1—2:3) is general; the second, particular. The move is from the cosmos to the garden. In the second account, humanity (not botany or astrology) is selected for further treatment. Just as in the first account there was mention of humankind in relation to God, humankind in relation to each other, and humankind in relation to the environment, so each of these themes now appears in the second account, with the elaboration of certain details and qualifications.

Each of the three relationships is further defined (and limited). As to the relationship between God and humankind, we hear of a new factor: obedience. Moreover, we hear a new note about the environment. While in the first account, God expressly stated that "every plant . . . and every tree which has fruit . . . shall be food for you" (Gen. 1:29), that mandate is now curtailed: they are not to eat the fruit from one tree (2:16-17). These two examples introduce other qualifications to the first account. We should be prepared for some refinement also in elaboration of the man/woman relationships. The account of the beginning of the family is given in the second half of the second creation account (2:18-24). Five observations/conclusions can be made from that treatment of man and woman.

First, man is given a lead responsibility for the environment. In Genesis 2 the subject of the environment is discussed solely in terms of Adam. Eve has not yet been formed. The garden is planted, and then "God took the man and put him into the garden of Eden to cultivate it and keep it" (Gen. 2:15). From the first account of creation we understand that the custody of the environment is a joint custody. But in the second account the responsibility is handed to the man in particular. Confirmation of such a conclusion comes from the Lord's word to Adam after the fall. The Lord tells Adam that the ground is cursed and that in toil shall he wrest food from the earth, for "both thorns and thistles it shall grow for you" (2:19). To Adam, more than to Eve, is the connection with the stewardship of the environment made. While the woman cannot escape responsibility for the environment, the man is responsible for "cultivating and keeping" the earth more particularly.

A second observation follows. In the story, the command to refrain from eating from the designated tree is given to the man even before the woman is formed (2:16). He is responsible for obedience. When Eve transgresses, with Adam close behind, the text notes that both hide themselves (3:11). In the story, God calls for the man, "Where are you?" (3:9). When Adam explains his fear and the reason for hiding, God addresses the man, "Who told you that you were naked? Have you eaten from the tree of which I commanded you not to eat?" (2:11). Only later in the conversation does God address himself to the woman. God fixes responsibility in Eden first on the man. The story makes clear that both are responsible, and both bear the consequences of their deed, but God gives the man primary responsibility.

Thirdly, the lead role for Adam is indicated by his task to assign names. The point of the passage is that by assigning names to the animals, Adam discerned distinctions among them, and in the process it became clear that no suitable helper for Adam was to be found among the animal species. A subsidiary point would not be missed by the Hebrews, for the responsibility of naming was held by someone with authority (Gen. 1:5, 8, 10; 17:5; 32:28; 2 Ki. 24:17). To name someone was indicative of authority.

In that garden setting, when the person formed by God was brought to him, Adam exclaimed, "She shall be called Woman, because she was taken out of Man" (Gen. 2:23). The woman's name is *Isshah* because she was taken from *Ish* (man). The joyous welcome accorded the woman is a comment on her importance; the designation of the name is in keeping with his position of lead responsibility.

A fourth observation turns around the expression "helper suitable for him" (2:18). As in English, so in Hebrew, the word "helper" signifies someone who comes along to assist. Some commentators have observed that the word in the Hebrew is often used of God, and have hinted that, using hierarchical language, this would mean that Eve, in this case, was to be over the man in importance. First, such a conclusion is quite out of keeping with the tenor of the passage. In the narrative, not so much as a statement or even any action is attributed to her. More important is the observation that Eve's role is in some way dependent upon Adam's. A woman writer is blunt: "She is made to be a cooperator as he is made to be an operator." To be sure God is a helper, but unlike Eve, his identity is not derived in terms of another.

Further, the "helper" was to be a complementary partner to Adam. The result of God's formative act of making woman out of man, was, judging by Adam's exclamation, totally satisfactory. Woman was indeed a complementary partner to man. Woman, so the apostle Paul asserts, was created for the sake of man (1 Cor. 11:9). Such a statement gives no license to chauvinists; both men and women exist from God and for God. Men have a primary responsibility; however, it is in view of this responsibility that woman is called alongside.

And that introduces a fifth observation. Adam is made first, then Eve. For moderns the order is decidedly less important than it was for ancient Israel. However, the laws of primogeniture, namely regulations governing the privileges and responsibilities of the firstborn, were carefully honored. In the genealogies of Genesis 5 the firstborn of each (except for Adam) is singled out and named.

Singular importance was given to the chronological priority of birth. That Ishmael, by virtue of being first, is entitled to the birthright is assumed. In an interesting complication with twins, Zerah, the first to appear, in the end is the last to be born, yet it is understood that Perez, the firstborn will be head of the clan (Gen. 38:27-30; cf. Gen. 46:12; Ruth 4:12, 18). So when Paul argues for male headship based on temporal priority ("For man does not originate from woman, but woman from man," 1 Cor. 11:8), he is consistent with the intention of the author of Genesis.

All five observations combined lead to the conclusion that a role differentiation between man and woman is imbedded in the creation order.   The man has a lead position. Significant in the argument for this contention is Paul's emphasis on the man's temporal priority (cf. 1 Tim. 2:13). The man cannot abdicate responsibility, even when it involves Eve. He has her for a helper; her identity is dependent on his vocation. This understanding of levels of responsibility—an understanding which cannot be detached from authority and accountability—has been the understanding for nearly two millennia of the church's teaching. If it needs correction, one can at least understand on what basis a preferred place was given to the man in the home and in the church.

The creation account ordering leads to two assertions. First, the conclusion, derived from the creation account in Genesis 1:1—2:3, is that man and woman are equal as persons. Secondly, the creation account of Genesis 2:4-24, while not subtracting in the least from the first assertion, points to a role differentiation, giving to the man a lead role. The two accounts must be taken together, otherwise distortion results. Those who seize on Genesis 2:4-24 to advocate male dominance over women are in error. Those who quote the passage about equality from Genesis 1 and fail to observe role differentiation as outlined in Genesis 2 are also in error. Indeed, the equality dimension is stressed first and last in the two accounts, perhaps so that the role differentiation found in the second account will not be overplayed. Male and female are in the image of God (1:27). "This is now bone of my bones, and flesh of my flesh" (Gen. 2:24), says Adam.   This "bracketing" of the material about man and woman is instructive because it asserts, first, the equality of the two; and given the story in Genesis 2, also the role differentiation that is to mark the two.

The divinely-ordained arrangement is a delicate balance. Men and women are equal ontologically (as things are in and of themselves), but God gave the man a primary responsibility. The roles of men and women are differentiated. That balance was upset in the fall. The differing roles now became a problem; there follows the so-called "battle of the sexes." The outcome of Eve's transgression was that the man would pervert his lead position and become arbitrary, harsh, and sometimes even tyrannical: "He shall rule over you" (Gen. 3:16). Likewise the woman, instead of acknowledging the husband's lead position, would seek to usurp his position: "Your desire shall be for your husband" (Gen. 3:16). This interpretation of "desire" as "desire to master" is defended, as scholars have noted, from the subsequent chapter where God addresses Cain, "Its [sin] desire is for you, but you must master it" (Gen. 4:7). The entrance of sin into the human race means that the appointed ordering would be abused and challenged.

TESTING THE PATTERN OF ORDERING
IN THE OLD TESTAMENT

The remainder of the Old Testament concurs with this kind of ordering—an ordering in which men and women are equal in worth, but in which functions are differentiated so that to men is given a lead role.

The strand of material in the Old Testament that asserts women's dignity is impressive. One can easily document examples of women's involvement and leadership. God makes a covenant with his people, men and women (Deut. 29:1-11). Women pray to God directly (Gen. 25:22-23) and minister before the Lord (Ex. 38:8). Miriam is part of the leadership team together with Aaron and Moses (Ex. 15:20-21); Deborah is a military commander (Judg. 4-5); Huldah a prophetess (2 Ki. 22:14); and Esther a queen. Wisdom, said to be with God at creation, is personified as a woman (Prov. 8). Such texts dare not be muffled; they proclaim the dignity that is accorded women. But to argue from these examples for role interchangeability is to ignore other texts— texts which are reminiscent of the creation ordering.

Old Testament texts that surface the lead position of men are so frequent that the patriarchy model is a large stumbling block to feminists. God's call is to Abram (Gen. 12); when he obeys he takes Sarai with him. The Torah stipulated that when women made vows, these were under the jurisdiction of fathers and husbands (Num. 30). However, for widows and divorced persons, every vow "shall stand" (Num. 30:9). Further evidence of the lead position of men is in the priesthood; there is no record that women were priests. The teaching and official cultic leadership function was denied them. A reason is not given. For that matter priesthood responsibilities were denied to all but the Levitical tribe, and even so only those over the age of thirty were eligible to be priests. It might be remembered that Miriam, chafing (along with Aaron) at Moses' leadership was not only rebuked but disciplined (Num. 12:9ff.). If one listens carefully to the Old Testament on this question of the role of women, one is impressed with the great latitude extended to women, but, consistent with Genesis 1—2, also with certain responsibilities deferred to men.

TESTING THE PATTERN OF ORDERING IN THE NEW TESTAMENT

Is the creation order which assigns a lead position to men overturned in the New Testament? Some argue that Christ's redemptive work effected a change in the fundamental ordering. They cite Galatians 3:28: "There is neither Jew nor Greek, there is neither slave nor free man, there is neither male nor female; for you are all one in Christ." In this passage which discusses the benefits of salvation, Paul insists that the barriers of gender and social class have tumbled down for those "in Christ." Such a statement is reminiscent of Genesis 1:27 which insists that as persons, both men and women are to be given full worth. To use this text as determinative for roles in ministry, however, is unwarranted because of the context. That question Paul addresses elsewhere.

In the early church the ministry of women was wideranging, to be sure. Women were among the disciples in the upper room (Acts 1:14). Lydia is mentioned (Acts 16:15), as are Philip's daughters who prophesy (Acts 21:8). Priscilla, along with her husband, instructs Apollos (Acts 18:26). Phoebe is listed as a servant-

minister (Rom. 16:1). In that same chapter Paul acknowledges the services of several women. Those who
urge these instances as reasons for role interchangeability, neglect another strand of texts, the so-
called restrictive texts.

These "restrictive texts" cannot here be exegeted in
detail; sketchy comments must suffice. In 1 Corinthians
11 Paul addresses worship. He says, "Christ is the head
of every man, and the man is the head of a woman, and
God is the head of Christ" (v. 3). Debate continues as to
whether "head" signifies authority, and is therefore hierarchical, or whether it can also mean source. Those who
have argued from Greek literature that "head" means
"source" are now being strongly challenged. The term
"head" is used for the source of a river, for example, but
also for its mouth. The conclusion is that head may also
mean "extremity." Though the word could mean
"source," it can hardly do so in this text for God is hardly the source of Christ. But that there is a structure—
call it hierarchical—is the plain sense of the text.
Without qualification, it is allowed by all Christians
that "Christ is the head of every man"—the first statement. Without qualification it is allowed by all believers
that "God is the head of Christ"—the third statement.
Why then is the in-between statement, "man is the head
of the woman," qualified and made to mean something
other than "hierarchical?"

The word "hierarchical" has by now a negative
meaning, no doubt because of the abuse by those who
have exercised authority irresponsibly. Another word
would be preferable. But the notion that in some sense
the man takes the lead (not towers above) is evident
from this text. Paul's teaching may not be reassuring either for men or for women, but to wiggle around the

text, or worse, to ignore it or even force an opposite meaning, is a procedure that cannot be condoned. To acknowledge a gradation of responsibility would be in keeping with the message of Genesis. Indeed in the same chapter, Paul, following the method of our Lord before him, appeals to the creation account. Paul argues his case noting that "man does not originate from woman, but woman from man" (1 Cor. 11:8).

Further insight into role differentiation comes from the same letter: "Let the women keep silent in the churches; for they are not permitted to speak, but let them subject themselves just as the Law also says" (1 Cor. 14:34). Here Paul appeals to Scripture. To read this text in the absolutist sense, however, as has been done by some hard-liners, is to ignore Paul's instructions in the same book for a woman who prays or prophesies (1 Cor. 11:5). Paul does not preclude the public ministry of women, but he circumscribes that ministry— corresponding with the creation ordering.

A similar explanation holds for the text in 1 Timothy 2. Paul instructs: "I do not allow a woman to teach or exercise authority over a man . . ." (1 Tim. 2:12). Yet women are to teach children (2 Tim. 1:5), teach other women (Tit. 2:3-4), and, in the case of Priscilla may on occasion teach men (Acts 18:26). The instructions to Timothy, some argue, pertain only to that situation in Ephesus and are not to be universalized to apply to all Christians. But that is questionable. Paul once more appeals to the creation order: "For it was Adam who was first created,and then Eve" (1 Tim. 2:13).

In summary, in Galatians Paul scores the point for women's equality with men. Such a position accords with Genesis 1. In 1 Corinthians 11 and 1 Timothy 2 Paul sets limitations for women in public ministry. Such

a position agrees with the creation account in Genesis 2.
There is a broad scope for ministry for women. However,
the conclusion is virtually inescapable that for Paul
some limitations are in effect.

Objections raised against this interpretation of the
man in lead position, revolve around two points: (1) giftedness, and (2) gender discrimination. It is argued, for
example, that it is irresponsible not to employ women's
gifts of leadership. A blunt reply is that as important as
women's gifts are, there are still parameters as to their
use. At issue is not the full deployment of gifts; at issue
is obedience to a divinely given pattern. Moreover it is
claimed that limitation of ministries for women is discrimination according to gender and that this is un-
worthy of the gospel. In reply one should note that entry into the kingdom for everyone means coming under
the lordship of Christ and that submission to him as
Lord is a non-negotiable requirement. In principle, ordering curbs freedom, for it means that "not everything
goes."

It must be underlined that submission, as the Bible
envisages it, does not of itself imply inferiority. When,
for example, an employee defers to his or her employer,
the issue is not an issue of intrinsic worth; the issue is
acknowledgement of role distinctions. The clincher for
this line of reasoning is to point to Jesus, the Son of
God. The Christian teaching is that Jesus is God and
that both God and Jesus are equal in deity. Still, it is
said of our Lord that he put himself at the service of
God the Father, and submitted to his will. In essence,
the two are equal; in function, one is submissive to the
other. So also in the man/woman relationship both in
the family and in church.

Does Christ reverse the results of the fall? Yes! As Paul explains, a husband's love is to be for his wife; a loving husband does not rule over his wife. Moreover, a Christian wife displays a submissive attitude to her husband. She is not about to usurp the role of her husband (cf. Gen. 3:16). The disharmony identified at the fall has been undone by Christ. Mutual submission is enjoined, and yet the role distinctions are observed. The creation order, which acknowledges levels of responsibility, remains. Otherwise, the statement that the husband is the head of the wife as Christ is the head of the church is a hollow paradigm. Carefully delineated symbols in Scripture should not be confounded.

CONCLUSION

To hold that in the creation pattern man and woman were accorded equal worth, but were assigned differentiated levels of responsibility, is to make sense of Paul's statements which, on the one hand, underscore the equality of the sexes, but on the other hand, delineate boundaries for roles. The practical application of such a theology needs further attention as to detail, but on the issue of women in ministry, the above exposition would mean a broad exercise of gifts for all—men and women. Clearly women, to whom dignity is to be accorded, have broad avenues for public ministry. At the same time it seems necessary that a respect for role differentiation be maintained. One might envision, for example, that women would preach, serve on boards, perhaps be ordained (given an understanding of ordination as affirmation, rather than entitlement to authority). But officially designated leadership roles, such as that of senior pastor, would be reserved for men. In what way the details of the above position would be expressed, given current organizations, needs further attention. The goal would be to express in a practical way, both the equality taught in Genesis 1 and the role differentiation noted in Genesis 2.

SUGGESTIONS FOR READING

Clark, Stephen B. Men and Woman in Christ: An Examination of the Roles of Men and Women in Light of Scripture and Social Sciences. Servant Books, 1980.

Foh, Susan T. "A Male Leadership View: The Head of the Woman Is the Man." Women in Ministry: Four Views, Bonnidell Clouse & Robert G. Clouse (eds.). InterVarsity Press, 1989: 69-105.

_____. Women and the Word of God: A Response to Biblical Feminism. Presbyterian and Reformed, 1980.

Hurley, James B. Man and Woman in Biblical Perspective. Zondervan, 1981.

Knight, George W. III. The Role Relationship of Men and Women: New Testament Teaching. Moody Press, 1985.

_____. New Testament Teaching on the Role Relationship of Men and Women. Baker, 1977.

Otwell, John H. And Sarah Laughed: the Status of Women in the Old Testament. Westminster, 1975.

Swartley, Willard M. Slavery, Sabbath, War, and Women: Case Issues in Biblical Interpretation. Herald Press, 1983.

EQUALITY OR
SUBORDINATION?   4

Allen Guenther

The Creation Account

Gladys Aylward, the unmarried missionary whose life-story, "The Small Woman," was made into a film, ex-pressed her insecurities about her famous ministry: "I wasn't God's first choice for what I've done for China. There was somebody else . . . I don't know who it was — God's first choice. It must have been a man — a wonderful man. A well-educated man. I don't know what happened. Perhaps he died. Perhaps he wasn't willing. . . . And God looked down . . . and saw Gladys Aylward." — Phyllis Thompson, <u>A Transparent Woman: The Compelling Story of Gladys Aylward</u>

Genesis 1—3 stands at the center of the Bible's teaching regarding the role and relationship of women and men. It is a foundational word which addresses all humanity.

Genesis 1 and 2 lead us to the original beauty of God's design — how we might be. From that original masterpiece, we can judge all attempts to express responses of faithful ministry among the people of God.

GENESIS 1:1—2:3

The Perspective

The account of creation is given from two interlocking perspectives. The first is recorded in Genesis 1:1—2:3. Here, in two parallel, three-day sequences, the writer pictures the creation of all things.

In the first three days God creates the world, separating it into its component parts (land, air, sea) and fixing their boundaries. The next three days God fills the earth with the moving beings and gives them the task of ruling over the spheres previously created.

The account takes us from the heavens to the earth, from the inorganic to the organic, from the lower forms of life to the highest form—people. The movement of thought points to people as the apex of creation. It is only after human beings (both male and female) have been created, and commissioned as God's representatives, that the world is said to be "very good." It is then that God rests from his creative work. The human beings are to carry out the remainder of the task under the blessing and supervision of the Almighty.

The Image of God

To fulfill that task, humans, unlike all other life forms, are made in "the form (image) and with the features (likeness) of God" (1:26). Unlike other creatures, of whom God made many kinds (1:20-22), God made only one kind of human (1:26-27). He made two of them (man and woman), but only one kind.

The alternation between the singular and plural, as well as the emphases on their being male and female and together being the image of God, are important aspects of the description:

> "Let **us** make [a] human in **our** image, having **our** features . . . . So God created the human in **his** own image. With **his** own features **he** created **him. He** created **them** male and female. Then God **(he)** blessed **them** and said to **them:** 'You (plural) have many children, so that you (plural) can fill the world and rule over all of it. Control all the fish. . .'" (vv. 26,27).

The retelling of this event in Genesis 5:1-2 adds the detail of their naming: "On the day God created a human, **he** made **him** with God's own features. **He** created **them** male and female. Then **he** blessed **them. He** also named **them** 'human' on the very day **he** created **them.**"

This alternation between singular and plural, with reference to both God and humans, suggests that male and female are together in the image of God and collectively share God's features. Alone, they cannot adequately reflect the image of God. Every reference to the "image" or "features [likeness]" is to the collective human [= 'adam], subsequently explained as creation of the male and female. Being male and female is an essential part of what it means to be like God. There is something unusual about people in that their sexuality reflects the nature of God implanted in them. In addition, the statement "let **us** make [a] human in **our** image," implies that their complementary nature reflects the social character of God.

The first picture of creation affirms that both male and female are given the mandate to procreate and to rule the life that has sprung from the earth at God's command. Neither is responsible to rule, control, or dominate the other. In fact, the world of people is excluded from the sphere of human dominion and rule.

Significantly, objections to the view of male and female as equals do not focus attention on Genesis 1. This passage clearly affirms the total equality of male and female. Not a syllable is uttered about role distinctions. Nothing is said about one ruling over the other. Together they are human; together they are in the likeness and bear the features of God.

GENESIS 2:4-25

Perspective of the Passage

Genesis 2:4-25 gives us a second snapshot of creation. An underlying argument connects the two accounts as follows. In Genesis 1, humans are presented as God's agents on earth to rule all animate life and the source (earth) from which it springs. Humans are the apex of creation. The world exists in total harmony only if humans supervise it. But if people are created last, then the whole world can exist, for a brief time at least, without humans. That would deny the essential role of people in maintaining the organic world in its right relationship to God. Therefore, this second creation snapshot shows God empowering people for their task and modeling the creation activity. Humans are shown how to rule over the plants (the Garden of Eden) and are pictured exercising authority over the animals (naming).

Verse 5 confirms this understanding of the passage. It cites two reasons for the lack of plant life: because God had not sent any rain, and because there was still

no person to do the work in the garden. The first deficiency was met by sending up a mist to water the soil
(v. 6); the second, by creating a person (v. 7). Having
made the point that the existence of people was essential to the well-being of all life on earth, the author
then proceeds to describe in detail the creation of all living beings **in the same order they are given in
Genesis 1:   plants, animals, and people (2:8ff.).**
Describing the creation of male and female in two different stages is necessary to point out that humans are essential for the proper functioning of the rest of the organic order. Without it, the two snapshots of creation
stand in conflict with one another.

The Creation of the Woman

The creation texts assume a male figure original.
The evidence for this lies in the words, "because she was
taken from a man" (v. 23b). Some interpreters contend
that we should see significance in Eve being created after Adam. But nowhere in Scripture is the argument
made that the husband is head of the family because
Adam was older than Eve, or because any other husband was older than his wife.

The man was created distinct from all other life
forms. Genesis 2:7 describes him as personally shaped
by God from the dust of the ground and infused with
life-giving breath. He stands apart from the animals on
both counts.

The woman is a clone with a difference. This unique
cloning operation suggests that the male human is incomplete, an incompleteness which cannot be addressed
by another male alone. That constitutes a strong statement in a patriarchal society where women were more
seen than heard, and where marriage was not known

primarily for companionship. Yet the text emphasizes the social rather than the reproductive function of the woman at this point. Presumably, God could have created multiple persons of the order of Adam by a means other than sexual intercourse. The animal world even now contains creatures (hermaphrodites) which possess both male and female organs.

The subsequent creation of the woman does not point to a lesser role for her (witness the mandate given equally to man and woman in Gen. 1). Nor can the fact that the man was created first be read as grounds for his authority over the animals and the woman, any more than the fact that the animals were created before the woman point to their superiority over her. Nor is the ground, created before all living beings, more important than the animals, plants, and people formed from it. Since woman is different than man, the text indicates that the essential identity (image of God) which characterizes them is clearly recognizable in both. Being male and female does not erase or diminish their essential identity with one another or their kinship with God.

The woman is created because "it is not good for the man to be alone" (2:16). She is God's solution to his incompleteness. She answers to his need by being a "helper who corresponds to him, one who is his counterpart." Strictly speaking, the word "help" used here refers to a person who has the capacity to help. A helper uniformly refers to someone, like God (16 out of 21 occurrences), who is stronger or has more resources than the person in need. It never refers to an assistant, an inferior, or one unrelated to the circumstances or condition for which the help is required. Woman's role as "helper" (by any interpretation of that word) indicates that she shares the tasks mandated by God.

When the man recognized the woman as his counterpart, he broke out in poetic ecstasy: "bone of my bone and flesh of my flesh" (2:23). This phrase appears elsewhere in the Old Testament as a reference to people who share a common bloodline or relationship (Judg. 9:2; 2 Sam. 5:1; 19:12,13). It is never used of children (minors), of descendants, or of subordinates. Instead, it is a claim or appeal by the speaker, for his/her own benefit, to equality of right or relationship (except in the case of Laban [Gen. 29:14], where it appears to be a statement of qualification for marriage). This phrase becomes a way of emphasizing the equality of the speaker and the person addressed.

Many interpreters have argued that Adam here names his wife, thereby accepting responsibility for her and exercising kindly authority over her. That interpretation, however, does not reflect a careful reading of the Hebrew. When a person names another, such as a child or a slave, an active verb is used (he named....). When, as in verse 23, the passive is used, the name refers to a nickname or a characterization by others to describe the person being referred to. This verse should, therefore, be translated, "people will call her woman" or "she will be called woman." In other words, the man does not name the woman. The passive (she will be called) is never used in the Scripture to describe the naming process by which a person asserts responsibility for, or authority over another. The act of naming the woman, by which the man asserts his authority over her, occurs only after the fall (3:20), thereby pointing to the naming as one of the consequences of the fall.

The Marital Relationship

The essential oneness of the two (bone of my bone; flesh of my flesh) in a special relationship is affirmed in marriage. The union of these two complementary persons (male and female) is sealed by a covenant, expressed in the words, "forsake" and "cling." "Forsake" speaks of a severing of one's primary tie in favor of another. The act is particularly significant when written to people in a culture where the tie to the parental home was strong. The original creation design was that the husband/wife relationship would become the primary tie of human relationships, setting aside the parent/child, child/parent, child/child, or individual/kinship group tie.

Every Israelite would have immediately noticed the unusual phrase, "therefore a man leaves his father and mother and clings (is glued) to his wife" (2:24). The woman does not get attached to the man's family as a possession or as an assistant. The man goes to her. That is particularly significant since Israelite couples lived with the husband's parents. But this text describes the husband as "leaving" his parental home and "being united" with his wife. The woman is the helper of the man. She now assumes the social role formerly held by his parents.

Genesis 2:4-25 contains no hint of superiority or inferiority of role distinctions, or of the loss of identity. Together, man and woman, both fully in God's image, are one whole in a way in which the man alone, or two men together, could not be.

GENESIS 3

Temptation and Fall

Throughout the centuries students of the Scriptures have puzzled over why Eve was approached by the serpent. We simply are not told. And since there are no clues, we do well to leave the question unanswered.

What we know is that the tempter stimulated in Eve the longing to be as God in respect to exercising independent moral judgments. The act of ruling requires decisions. "Knowing good and evil" is the quality whereby people make mature moral judgments. The woman wanted to make self-determined decisions. This act of disobedience represents the short-cut to moral maturity. It is a grasping for the Creator's power by the one appointed to represent God.

The text indicates that Eve was deceived (3:1,13) and hints that Adam sinned knowingly (3:6). The difference between "sins of the moment" (Lev. 22:14; Num. 35:9,15; Deut. 4:42; 19:4; Josh. 20:3,5,9) and "sins committed with a high hand" (deliberately, exultantly; cf. Num. 33:3; Deut. 19:11) is important. Those designations appear in Israel's legislative literature to distinguish between one who has committed manslaughter and one who is a murderer. The willful sin merits the death penalty; the unwitting sin does not. That makes Adam the more accountable sinner. That is why he is addressed first, not because he is the representative of the family.

Consequences and Curses

It is important to note the effects of the fall on human relationships. Our present experiences are not representative of God's design for redemptive restoration.

Since redemption represents a restoration to harmony as God initially created humanity, it should lead us back to Genesis 1,2 (not chs. 3ff.) as the norm for understanding the ministry of men and women in the divine economy. Those who are being recreated in the divine image are freed from the power of sin, even though the consequences of sin remain very much apparent in people of faith as well as in the world. But God's work of salvation reverses the effects of the fall through Christ's victory over death and Satan, and by breaking the stranglehold of the powers of this age. One of those powers is the frequent domination of men over women.

The first sin brought with it a tidal wave of consequences. The new self-understanding of Adam and Eve was mixed with shame and fear of self-disclosure, followed by their refusal to acknowledge responsibility and by mutual accusations. But God would have none of it. He addresses each as an independent moral agent. He addresses the man first, however, since his sin was the greater and worthy of greater punishment. God issues the curses in the reverse order to the call of accountability, namely, on the serpent, the woman, and the man. The final stages of punishment—acts of grace as well as judgment—are expulsion from the garden and death (3:22-24; 5:4ff.).

Eve is cursed in the realm of childbearing, Adam in tilling the ground. Why does the text distinguish between the two in terms of the two aspects of the creation mandate of 1:26-30? Did women not work the fields? Did men not have a role in begetting and rearing children? Of course! The reason for this separation and distinction is unclear. It was not present in the original mandate. In the case of Adam, the connection with the soil is linked to his being uniquely formed from the soil. In the case of Eve, the act of childbearing is connected to her unique contribution to their joint calling. Both share in each aspect of the creation mandate; each experiences the pain most sharply in one dimension.

The meaning of "Eve's desire" has attracted considerable attention because it bears upon the issue of the woman's subordination or equality. If we read *teshuqah* as "sexual desire" (cf. Canticles 7:10), the divine decree on the woman means that her sexual longing for her husband will supersede her fear of the pain of bearing children. But this reading of the text does not clarify how and why the man should/would rule over her. On the other hand, a comparison of these words with God's reproof of Cain (Gen. 4:7) suggests quite another meaning for *teshuqah*. In 4:7 God confronts Cain for being angry because God has not accepted Cain's cavalier attitude in bringing an inferior sacrifice. The confrontation includes the words, "Isn't it the case that if you had done the right thing, you would be smiling, but since you have not done the right thing, sin is crouching at your door."

Its desire (is) for you
but you will/shall rule over it.

The comparable text with regard to Eve (3:16), says:

Your desire (is) for your husband
but he will/shall rule over you.

The parallel is too perfect to be coincidental. The construction of the two sentences is identical. The only difference between them is in the referent of the pronouns. Genesis 4:7 indicates that an acceptable translation of *teshuqah* is "desire to rule or to dominate," especially in view of the fact that the line ends with the concept of ruling. If we accept this translation, Genesis 3:16 introduces us to the battle between the sexes. As a consequence of the fall, women will attempt to dominate their husbands, but the males will forcefully assert their rule (domination) over women.

This latter interpretation also does justice to the parallel to the curses spoken against the serpent and Adam. In each case hostility has sprung to life. In the first instance, the conflict erupts between the serpent and the woman (and her descendants). In the second, it invades the marriage and creates disharmony, with the man becoming dominant. In the third instance, the curse brings the earth into revolt against the man. The task of ruling is made immeasurably more difficult, only to result in a return to the very soil from which the man came. The winner of each round becomes the loser of the next.

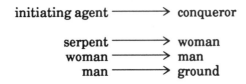

A perversion has occurred. In failing to heed God's command, every domain of life has become the scene of major conflict.

The implication is that the domination of the female by the male is a result of the fall. Such domination, it suggests, is the inevitable course of events in a sinful world, but it does not represent God's original intention. Since God's redemptive plan is to reverse the consequences of the fall—to remake us in his image—to continue male domination is to deny the reconciling work of God in the relationship between the sexes.

IMPLICATIONS FOR MINISTRY

Genesis 1 teaches the equality and complementarity of women and men in their being and their calling. Arguments drawn from Genesis 2—3 for the subordination of women cannot be sustained. While it is true that Eve fell into sin first, why should that restrict the ministry of women? The man's sin was the more severe. If anyone's ministry were to be restricted, it should be his.

Clearly, arguments against the full and equal ministry of women cannot be sustained from Genesis 1—3. Instead, these chapters affirm the complementary character of man and woman and their full equality in the mandate to rule the created order and to procreate and fill the earth with offspring. The issues of power and control were introduced in the fall. The man's domination of the woman over the centuries is the result of fallenness, not the result of being in God's image or in any mandate given to him. The woman's attempts at domination are equally the result of fallenness. At its very least, redemption addresses that perversion, making men and women capable of ministering to one another through the gifts and according to the calling of God.

SUGGESTIONS FOR READING

Bilezikian, Gilbert. Beyond Sex Roles. Baker, 1985.

Clark, Stephen B. Man and Woman in Christ. Servant Books, 1980.

Evans, Mary J. Woman in the Bible. InterVarsity, 1983.

Foh, Susan. "What Is the Woman's Desire." <u>Westminister Theological Journal</u> 37 (1975): 376-383.

Hurley, James B. <u>Man and Woman in Biblical Perspective</u>. Zondervan, 1981.

Lorraine E. Matties
Gordon H. Matties

Old Testament Perspectives on the Ministry of Women

In 621 B.C., while renovating the Temple, King Josiah's workers discovered a scroll of the law. When Josiah read the scroll he was horrified. The people of Judah were unfaithful to God's commands. He sent five advisors to consult the Lord about the teachings of the scroll. The advisors went straight to Huldah, a prophetess. Her message from the Lord was clear: "I am going to punish Jerusalem and all its people, as written in the book that the King has read." — 2 Kings 22

We can learn much about God and his people in the Old Testament's narratives, laws, poetry and prophetic writings. We must be careful, however, to distinguish between our culture and theirs when we apply Old Testament stories and laws to our situations. Traditions and social laws have changed, but God was clearly working to redeem the Israelite people in the midst of their culture, even as he is working to redeem the world today.

OLD TESTAMENT CULTURAL PERSPECTIVES

Although the creation accounts in Genesis indicate that God's image is reflected in both male and female (see Ch. 4), God is consistently referred to with masculine pronouns. That was not unusual in a society that often ignored women altogether. But a careful reading of the Old Testament shows that the images used to describe God include both female and male characteristics. Beside the many masculine metaphors of God, such as husband, warrior, and king, stand images that refer to the maternal qualities of giving birth, nurturing and protecting (Num. 11:11-12; Deut. 32:18; Ps. 22:9-10; Isa. 42:14; 46:3-4; 49:15; 63:15-16; Jer. 31:20, 22; Hos. 2:16, 21). Such multiple images are evidence that God's identity was not defined solely by the male gender.

Moreover, Israel rejected the sexually-based deities of the ancient world. In distinction from other ancient Near-Eastern religions, whose gods and goddesses were explicitly linked with sexuality through fertility rites, the God of Israel was known as creator, nourisher, and sustainer. God's nature was expressed through authentic and just relationships, not in the manipulation of the universe through sexual ritual. For that reason, the Israelites abhorred the imitation of the gods through sexual activity or in sacred prostitution. They regarded the human family as sacred and preserved it by refusing to link sexual activity with the divine/human relationship.

Ideally, that fact should have offered women a more prominent place of dignity, and indeed, the Israelites regarded motherhood highly. But the reality for women apart from that role most often fell short of the ideal. For the most part, women were dependent on and subordinate to their fathers before marriage, and to their husbands afterward. A wife was expected to uphold her husband's dignity by maintaining his household and bearing children, preferably sons. The fate of women outside those prescribed positions was often precarious, even desperate. A number of stories tell of women being brutally mistreated by their male masters, with no record of punishment for the crime (e.g., Gen. 19:1-11; Judg. 19).

Israelite culture was clearly male-dominated. Leadership positions were primarily filled by men, although there were some notable exceptions.

THE PRIESTHOOD

The priesthood is the clearest example of male leadership. It was reserved for male descendants of Aaron. All others, including women, were excluded from that office. Since God was not understood as a sexual being, however, the reason for the exclusion of women from the priesthood must be found elsewhere. Some have suggested the ritual uncleanness of women (because of the menstrual cycle and childbirth) as a reason for exclusion, but this is not satisfactory. A whole range of reasons for ritual impurity prevented both males and females from service in worship at various times (e.g., Lev. 15).

The Old Testament offers no explanation for the choice of Aaron's descendants as priests. Many scholars have suggested that men and women serving together in the temple rites was a problem because of pagan religious practices in which the worshipers used sexual activity to influence the gods.

The example of the male priesthood in Israel cannot be used to argue the exclusion of women from leadership in the church. Three arguments prohibit such a conclusion. First, the priestly role was hereditary. Only the Levites from the family of Aaron were eligible. The restrictions on priestly eligibility eliminated most men as well as all women. There is no corresponding priestly family in the church from which leadership is drawn.

Secondly, public leadership in Israel was not limited to the priestly family. Judges, kings, and prophets were also leaders who gave leadership in religious rites, covenant renewal, administration, and teaching. Women were included in the ranks of judges, royalty, and prophets.

Thirdly, and most compelling, the New Testament never defines church leadership roles in terms of the Old Testament priesthood. On the contrary, the New Testament depicts all God's people as priests (e.g., 1 Pet. 2:4-10). The only Old Testament leadership role that persists as a leadership ministry in the church is prophecy. None of the leadership lists in the New Testament mentions priesthood as a ministry (cf. Rom. 12:1-8; 1 Cor. 12-14; Eph. 4:1-16). The priesthood is not a model for leadership in the church. Therefore, its restrictions cannot apply to leadership in the church.

OLD TESTAMENT WOMEN IN MINISTRY

What did ministry mean for women in ancient Israel? Although the majority of Old Testament texts

about women place them in roles of subordination, there
are exceptions that indicate that the prevailing attitudes toward women were not the only ones, or the
ideal ones.

Women and the Law

Israelite law reveals God's plan for the people of
Israel. The covenant is consistent with God's character,
and yet reflects the limitations of particular cultural settings. Many examples can be cited to show that Israelite
law did not afford complete equality to both men and
women. Israelite law was addressed to men. In fact,
since a woman was part of the man's household, the law
did not always distinguish her from his material posses-
sions (cf. Ex. 20:17; Deut. 5:21). One of the many laws
that favored men over women allowed a husband to accuse his wife of infidelity, and to submit her to a testing
ordeal (Num. 5:11-31). Women had no similar right.
Except in their role as mother, women were always inferior to and dependent on men.

We must understand woman's legal status, however,
in terms of how law functioned within the larger social
patterns in Israel. In relation to the cultural context,
law preserved and fostered order in society. But more
importantly, Israelite law was intended to assure the in-
tegrity, stability, and economic viability of the family as
the basic unit of society. In most cases, the interests of
the family were identified with its male head. His rights
and duties were described with respect to other men and
their property.

In spite of the Israelite woman's subordinate role,
some women acted independently of men to ensure their
own security. The daughters of Lot (Gen. 19:30-38);
Tamar, the daughter-in-law of Judah (Gen. 38); and

Ruth and Naomi all took the initiative to preserve the high law of family solidarity even when performing questionable actions. Hannah vowed to give her son to the Lord (1 Sam. 1:11; cf. Num. 30:3-15) even before she was pregnant, apparently without concern for the law that said her husband could revoke her vows because of the priority of family interests.

Yet even within the Old Testament legal literature an openness to change is evident. In Numbers 27 the daughters of Zelophehad ask Moses to change the inheritance laws so that they can inherit their father's property. Moses, after consulting with God, allows their request. In Numbers 36, however, a group of clan leaders (men) suggest to Moses that the new law could endanger the landholdings of the tribe if the daughters married outside the tribe. In response, Moses decrees that a daughter who inherits her father's property may marry only within his tribe (Num. 36:6-9). This example shows how case law developed in ancient Israel. More importantly, it shows that women were able to raise issues publicly that affected their status. The texts show that Israelite law was flexible and adaptable to new situations. It is interesting to note the way in which the biblical record reflects Israel's continuing interpretation of God's will for new situations (e.g., Deut. 15:12 revises Ex. 21:2-11).

Women and Wisdom

For the most part, women are depicted in the Book of Proverbs in the roles of mother and wife. The proverbs praise the gracious and prudent wife who enhances her husband's reputation (12:4) and repudiates the wife who is contentious and brings shame on her husband (19:13; 21:9; 25:4; 27:15-16). As mothers, women are shown to be teachers alongside their husbands (1:8; 6:20; 23:22), except in Proverbs 31:1-9 where their activities are seen as independent. The exceptional woman of Proverbs 31:10-31 is a model of a woman who is engaged in all manner of economic and social activity, who cares for her family and ministers to the needy.

The most important feature about the role of women in the Book of Proverbs is the personification of woman as wisdom and folly (especially in Prov. 1—9). Proverbs 8 clearly shows that wisdom is closely associated with God as a unique presence or principle of God's activity at creation. Hence, the exceptional woman of Proverbs 31 reflects the embodiment of wisdom in the life of a woman. Thus, although the proverbs themselves functioned primarily as instruction to young men, the Book of Proverbs offered women a model to follow—the personification of divine wisdom.

Several women associated with David exemplify this practical application of wisdom in the public sphere. Two unnamed "wise" women are involved in diplomatic activity during his reign; the people recognized a wise woman from Tekoa (2 Sam. 14:1-24), and another from the city of Abel (2 Sam. 20) as skillful negotiators. The fact that David's general Joab engaged their services suggests that the women had leadership positions in their cities.

Similarly, before David becomes king, Abigail acts wisely to cover for her foolish husband (who happens to be named Nabal, meaning "fool"; 1 Sam. 24). Although she is not called a "wise woman," as the others were, she fulfilled the role of the diplomatic and perceptive wise woman who is able to act decisively in difficult political situations.

Women and Prophecy

Several Old Testament women were called prophets, the most important office in Israel. The prophet represented the King of Heaven. He or she was the "voice" of God communicating God's will for the present to the Israelite community. Through prophets God appointed and deposed kings and criticized other leaders who acted contrary to his will. Prophecy offered a critique of the people's attempts to master their own destiny, and announced new alternatives for redemption and liberation.

In the period before the monarchy, two women stood out as prophets: Miriam, the sister of Aaron (Ex. 15:20), and Deborah (Judg. 4:4). Miriam demonstrated her leadership when she dared to accuse Moses of his exclusive claim to the word of God. Although the people criticized Miriam for challenging Moses' unique relationship to God, the prophet Micah remembers her as one of the three great leaders of the exodus era (Mic. 6:4).

Deborah, who also performed the tasks of a judge, was a politician and strategist. She received an oracle from God and passed the orders on to Barak. No one questioned the validity of her role as an agent of God's word. The poetic compositions of Miriam and Deborah are among the few biblical passages thought to have been composed by women (Ex. 15:20-21; Judg. 5).

The story at the beginning of this chapter reports how King Josiah sent some of his officials to consult the prophetess Huldah concerning the validity of the book of the law discovered during the temple renovations (2 Ki. 22:8-20; 2 Chron. 34:14-28). Huldah's word from God confirmed the authenticity of the law book. Her activity was no different from that of male prophets. That Josiah would consult a woman at all makes her story remarkable since both Jeremiah and Zephaniah were acting as prophets at that time.

Ezekiel (13:17-23) and Nehemiah (6:14) condemned other prophetesses as false prophets, not because they were women but because they were opposing the will of God.

The most fascinating dimension of women's relation to prophecy in the Old Testament is the vision of Joel about the last days (2:28-29). This text, cited in Peter's Pentecost sermon (Acts 2:17), reflects an understanding that God's desire for humanity is larger than any cultural limitations. Although both men and women could be prophets, few women were able to break through the barriers of patriarchal social norms. Joel, however, envisioned a time when they would not have to struggle against cultural restrictions, for God would define what was possible for humanity. Although Acts 2:17 may well echo the hope of Joel, his vision is still awaiting its complete realization (see also the puzzling passage in Jer. 31:21-22).

Other Women in the Historical Narratives

Besides the women who are remembered for their public ministry, other women also figure prominently in the narratives of the Old Testament. Narrative (history and story) functions to explain the world as it is experienced and to invite readers to make responsible choices for the future. Women are sometimes depicted in this literature as colorful personalities, sometimes as abused victims, sometimes as responsible wives and mothers, and sometimes as near legendary heroines. Yet women are rarely the center of attention. Most often they fulfill supporting roles to men. Several of these women deserve mention, not so much because they engaged in public ministry, or because they were leaders in Israel, but because they were models of faithfulness, which is ultimately the most important ministry of all.

Through their faithfulness these women are often the hidden agents of God's redemptive activity. For example, the matriarchs of Genesis, although usually concerned with domestic affairs, sometimes take it upon themselves to ensure that God's will is accomplished despite the interests of powerful men. Rebekah secretly arranged for Jacob to receive Isaac's blessing (Gen. 27). She also initiated a reconciliation between the estranged brothers, Jacob and Esau (Gen. 27:41-45). The Hebrew midwives in Egypt, Shiphrah and Puah, along with Moses' mother and sister, dared to defy Pharaoh's orders that all male children be killed (Ex. 1:15-2:10). Bathsheba and Esther played significant roles in royal courts even though queens and queen mothers were not common in the ancient world (1 Ki. 1:15-21; 2:19-20; Esther).

Three final comments round out this survey. First, even when women suffered at the hands of others, they were paid special attention by God. God visited Hagar, Abraham's concubine, in the desert. She was promised a child, and in reply she rightly exclaimed her surprise at having seen God (Gen. 16:7-13). Later, after she had been expelled by Abraham and was near death in the desert, God came to her and her son Ishmael and promised to make a nation of their descendants (Gen. 21:8-21).

Second, women were sometimes the ones who most perceptively recognized the hand of God in current events. That is most obvious in the Book of Joshua, where a woman was among the few to acknowledge that God was with Israel (e.g., Rahab in Josh. 2).

Third, it is noteworthy that no criticism is ever directed against women's public roles in Israelite or non-Israelite societies by the writers of the Old Testament. Priests who do not fulfill their obligations are condemned. False prophets are judged. Unjust judges and kings are denounced. But nowhere do the Old Testament writers express their or God's disapproval of women in leadership roles. They were not seen as transgressing in a male-only domain.

CONCLUSION

There is a predominance of male leadership in the Old Testament. How do we explain this pattern? At least three factors are involved. The first is patriarchy. A patriarchal society does not necessarily exclude female leadership (other ancient Near-Eastern societies were patriarchal and had prophetesses, priestesses, and queens), but it defines identity through the family line of the male. Women usually married in their early teens, surrendered their own power by entering the husband's family structure, and were confined to the home to bear children and care for the family. Women rarely became public figures in patriarchal societies. Secondly, formal education was restricted to males. Women were not prepared for leadership roles in public or religious service. Thirdly, the priesthood was restricted to male descendants of Aaron. This excluded most men as well as all women. We are given no reasons for God's choice in this matter.

But even these powerful forces did not exclude women from leadership roles in Israel. The exceptional leadership of women such as Miriam, Deborah, and the wise women of Tekoa and Abel suggest that anyone could serve in recognized positions of leadership. The Israelites clearly acknowledged wisdom and prophecy as gifts from God to men and women for private and public service.

Ministry cannot, of course, be limited to positions of leadership. This is shown by the prominence of women in family life, where they were sometimes considered superior to men in their wisdom and ability to make decisions that affected the destiny not only of the family, but of the people of Israel as well. Similarly, women were respected as mothers just as men were respected as fathers (Deut. 5:12). Mothers and fathers were equally responsible for the nurture of children, and for instruction in wisdom. So also the Song of Songs illustrates that women were ideally equal partners in the sexual relationship. Although Israel's practice did not often reflect these possibilities and ideals, the Old Testament testifies to a vision of mutuality and equality toward which God is moving his people. God's spirit or wisdom can rest on any individual, male or female. If we choose to participate in God's continuing work of redemption, we will find ourselves moving toward that vision.

Even though men were more prominent in Israel's leadership, women were never criticized for offering the gifts that God had given them. In the entire Old Testament only the Song of Songs alludes to the curse of subordination in Genesis 3:16, and in doing so the writer transforms a negative image into a positive one of mutuality (7:10).

No writer in the Old Testament ever advocates the subordination of women based on Genesis 3. The creation order is never mentioned as the basis for theological viewpoints or practice with regard to the place of women in Israel. In contrast, however, women are mentioned as participants in the hope of God's coming rule. There is, therefore, a correspondence between the creation ideal and the redemptive vision of God's coming kingdom. That vision, and not the social pressures that forced women to serve in a subservient capacity, ought to be the clue that guides Christians in understanding the Old Testament.

Above all, the prophets envision women as well as men as bearers of the Spirit of God, with whom all things are possible. God's design for redemption is directed toward the mutuality of the sexes. The goal of creation is a new humanity—male and female—a community of equal redemptive agents in a broken world. For women in particular, the Old Testament witness demonstrates that women are neither restricted nor exempt from answering God's call to ministry in all its various forms, regardless of the limitations a society may impose.

SUGGESTIONS FOR READING

Bird, Phyllis. "Images of Women in the Old Testament," The Bible and Liberation: Political and Social Hermeneutics. Ed. N.K. Gottwald. Orbis Books, 1983. 252-288.

Brenner, Athalya. The Israelite Woman: Social Role and Literary Type in Biblical Narrative. JSOT Press, 1985.

Evans, Mary J. Woman in the Bible. InterVarsity Press, 1983.

Myers, Carol. "The Roots of Restriction: Women in Early Israel." Biblical Archeologist 41 (1978): 91-103.

Scalise, Pamela J. "Women in Ministry: Reclaiming our Old Testament Heritage." Review and Expositor 83 (1986): 7-13.

Strom, Donna. "Where Are the Deborahs and Baraks?" Evangelical Review of Theology 10 (1986): 19-26.

Swidler, Leonard. Biblical Affirmations of Women. Westminster Press, 1979.

Trible, Phyllis. God and the Rhetoric of Sexuality. Fortress Press, 1978.

Timothy Geddert

A New Vision for Humanity

> *With the possible exception of the angel's announce-*
> *ment of the coming conception, the scriptural record*
> *never shows us Mary at home. She is hurrying off to*
> *Elizabeth, then going to Bethlehem for the census, then*
> *to Jerusalem for purification rites, down to Egypt,*
> *back to Nazareth, then to Jerusalem again for*
> *Passover, to Cana for the wedding, to Capernaum, to a*
> *city near the Sea of Galilee with her other sons to per-*
> *suade Jesus to come home, and finally to Jerusalem*
> *again. — Dorothy A. Pape, <u>In Search of God's Ideal</u>*
> <u>Woman</u>

Jesus lived in an age of sexual discrimination. Women were the objects of abuse and dehumanization. Most were barred from full participation in public life and from leadership roles in Jewish religion.

Twentieth-century Christians disagree whether women are to be excluded from certain leadership roles because of their sex. Those who say some leadership roles are divinely ordained to be filled only by men would deny that the issue is sexual discrimination. The issue is rather "creation order" (see Ch. 3). Those who believe that women should participate fully at all levels of church ministry and leadership see the exclusion of women from some ministry roles as a form of sexual discrimination.

These two issues (discrimination and exclusion) were, in fact, two sides of the same coin in first-century Palestine. The radical way in which Jesus related to women dealt with both issues at the same time and has important implications for the contemporary church seeking to live out Jesus' vision for humanity.

A MAN OUT OF STEP WITH HIS WORLD

Jesus, though divine, knew how to relate to humankind; though righteous, how to relate to sinners; though king of kings, how to relate to common people; and though a man, how to relate to women. Dorothy Sayers in Are Women Human? writes:

> They [women] had never known a man like this Man — there never has been such another. A prophet and teacher who never nagged at them, never flattered or coaxed or patronized; who never made arch jokes about them, never treated them either as "The women, God help us!" or "The ladies, God bless them!"; who rebuked without querulousness and praised without condescension; who took their questions and arguments seriously; who never mapped out their sphere for them, never urged them to be feminine or jeered at them for being female; who had no axe to grind and no uneasy male dignity to defend... (p. 47).

Jesus' way of relating to women contrasted sharply with the rabbis' way. Their approach was to foster attitudes and introduce legislation designed to keep women out of public life as far as possible. In their eyes, women had two primary roles: to raise children for their husbands, and to satisfy their husband's sexual desires lest he satisfy them immorally elsewhere. No rabbi would have had women disciples, and some Jewish religious groups shunned the company of women altogether.

In contrast to the rabbis, Jesus related openly and naturally with women of all sorts, respectable and immoral (Lk. 7:37; 8:2,3; Jn. 4:17,18), "clean" and "unclean" (Mk. 5:30-34). He touched them (Mk. 1:31) and let them touch him (Lk. 7:39). He even defended a sinful woman for kissing him in public (Lk. 7:45-47)!

Women were also a part of the entourage that followed Jesus as he traveled around the country ministering to the crowds (Lk. 8:1-3). Not only did women accompany him, they ministered to him (Mk. 15:41), with him (Lk. 8:1-3), and for him (Jn. 4:28-30, 39-42).

Jesus openly engaged in theological discussions with women (Jn. 4:7-26; 11:21-27; Mk. 7:24-29), something no rabbi of the first century would have considered. He entrusted some of his most important self-revelations to women. To the woman at the well he revealed himself as Christ [Messiah] and "I am" [i.e., Yahweh] (cf. Jn. 4:25,26). To Martha he revealed himself as the resurrection and the life (Jn. 11:25). In return, women were among those who most clearly understood his identity (Jn. 11:27) and his mission (Mk. 14:3-9). Interestingly, the resurrection message was first entrusted to women by the angel who commissioned them to tell the male disciples (Mk. 16:7; Jn. 20:18-20).

In Luke 10:38-41 Jesus chides Martha for being distracted with the meal preparations and affirms her sister Mary who "sat at the Lord's feet." The incident is much more than a call to value the contemplative life over the active. It is a clear endorsement of theological education for women. Mary had taken the posture of a rabbi's disciple. Jesus implicitly invites Martha to join her there.

PRINCIPLES THAT SHAPED JESUS' WAY OF RELATING TO WOMEN

What vision motivated Jesus to relate to women as he did? Jesus' mission was to usher in God's Kingdom, a kingdom defined as "doing God's will on earth, as it is done in heaven" (Mt. 6:10). His mission was to act out God's will in all things and to call and prepare followers to do the same. This meant living by principles that were at odds with his contemporaries. What principles influenced the way Jesus related to people and to women in particular?

Jesus Related to People as People
We are accustomed to defining "male" and "female" in terms of their respective roles in the home, society, and the church. People living in the first century did so even more sharply. Jesus' startling contribution was not to take the "feminine role" and modify it. Instead, he ignored it! Some may object to this statement on the grounds that he chose only men as his twelve official disciples. It is true that only men were selected for this role and we must assess the significance of this fact. But apart from his selection of apostles, it is impossible to detect any difference between the way Jesus treated men and the way he treated women.

Jesus consistently lessened the significance of religious status, social standing, and economic situation.
For Jesus, religious status counted for nothing and its
lack was not a deficiency. Wealth did not increase one's
worth nor poverty decrease it. The handicapped were as
important as the able-bodied, the servant as important
as the master, the child as important as the parent. If
Jesus made any "class" distinctions at all, it was to engage in affirmative action, helping the underprivileged,
the marginalized, and the oppressed gain what society
denied them.

Jesus clearly looked beyond his own race, nation,
and gender. Throughout his ministry, and decisively
through his death, Jesus prepared the way so that
Gentiles could be members alongside and equal to Jews
in God's new humanity. By his actions, Jesus showed
that a woman has an intrinsic value just as great as
that of a man. For Jesus, the equality of male and female was not a distant goal; it was a self-evident fact.

Jesus worked in a variety of ways to eliminate strictly enforced differences of role based on gender. He gave
women public roles unheard of in their society; and
when men fought for authority and honor he called
them to accept precisely that to which first-century
women were normally consigned — servanthood. He
practiced it supremely himself (Mk. 10:35-45).

Jesus Dealt with the Root Cause of Sexual Discrimination

One of the main reasons women were the objects of
sexual discrimination in first-century Palestine was
that men viewed them first and foremost as sexual beings, not as human beings. Jesus reversed that priority.

He attacked the problem of sexual discrimination at its root, male lust.

First-century rabbis blamed women for most immoral sexual behavior (see Jn. 8:3-6). Women were seen as temptresses. The solution was to keep women out of public life (so that men would not be tempted) and in the home (where a woman could satisfy her husband's sexual desires).

Jesus agreed with the Jewish rabbis that lust is wrong, but he disagreed that it was inevitable in the presence of a woman. When Jesus said, "Anyone who looks at a woman lustfully has adulterated her already in his heart" (Mt. 5:28), he did much more than move the basis of adultery from open actions to hidden thoughts. He provided a radically new solution to the problem of lust. Adultery was to be prevented by making men responsible for their own lustful thoughts, not by removing women from their sight.

Lust is inevitable for men if women are viewed first and foremost as sexual beings whose primary function is to satisfy men's sexual desire. It is deliberate sin if women are first and foremost human beings made in God's image.

Jesus Made Family Relationships Subordinate to Kingdom Work

In the first century, a woman was defined almost exclusively in terms of her family relations. One day a Jewish woman called out to Jesus, "Blessed is the mother who gave birth and nursed you" (Lk. 11:27). Jesus countered with "Blessed rather are those who hear the word of God and obey it" (11:28). Jesus made it clear that a woman's status and blessedness do not depend on the children she bears, however great they may be. He also clearly implied that when a woman orders the priorities of her life, she must never rank motherhood higher than kingdom work. But Jesus went even further. He declared that his own mother, the one whom this unnamed Jewess called "blessed," could not be considered a member of Jesus' true family unless she qualified, not by physical parenthood, but by her own obedience to God's will (Mk. 3:31-35).

Women, like men, are blessed if they hear God's word and obey. When Jesus looked down from his cross and declared to Mary and John, "Behold your son—behold your mother" (Jn. 19:25-27), he was not merely caring for his physical mother. He was defining his spiritual family. Mary and John, a woman and a man, stand there as models of discipleship and members of a spiritual family because they heard God's word and obeyed. They followed Jesus to his cross.

Jesus Refused to Accept the Fallen World as Normal

No aspect of Jesus' vision has such far-reaching implications as the fact that he simply refused to accept the fallen conditions of this world as normal.

According to the rabbis, if men normally look on women lustfully, women should be excluded from public life. Jesus refused to accept what was common as the norm. The ideal is the norm, not common behavior.

Jesus used the same approach when asked what grounds made divorce legitimate (Mk. 12:18-27). His questioners assumed that the fallen world was the norm and that its failures had to be reckoned with and controlled. Jesus said that God's original intention at creation is the norm. The kingdom of God is not defined as humans doing their own will in the least destructive way. It is defined as humans doing God's will on earth as it is done in heaven. The ideal is the norm.

Clearly we live in a fallen world, and Jesus knew that better than any of us. In a fallen world we need guidelines to help regulate our affairs, but Jesus refused to accept the fallen world as the norm. Many of his teachings appear foolish when evaluated by the standards of this world. The problem is with the world, not with Jesus' vision of the kingdom.

JESUS' EARLIEST FOLLOWERS
CATCH THE VISION

Jesus' own attitude to the question of gender relations was significantly affected by his "other-worldly" vision. He called his followers to fix their eyes on a kingdom in which the child, the servant, and women provide models of greatness. He called humanity to look back to the time before sin corrupted them and to see God's creative design. He called humanity to look forward past their final redemption to see themselves and each other as they were destined finally to be. He called humanity to look around and see God's will coming to pass on earth as it already operated in heaven. He called his followers to live by his vision of the kingdom.

The gospel writers were among the first to catch the vision. We know that because they passed on the stories about Jesus' revolutionary way of treating humanity, and women in particular. But we also know it because they structured their gospel accounts in ways which challenge the discerning reader to catch the vision, especially with regard to gender relations.

At strategic points in his narrative, Mark places stories of women who practiced active faith (5:25-34; 7:25-

30) and self-denying service (12:41-44; 14:3-9) to contrast uncomprehending, faithless, self-seeking men (cf. esp. 4:40; 8:21; 9:32; 9:33,34; 10:35-37; 13:1,2; 14:50).

It has long been recognized that Luke highlights Jesus' interaction with women. In at least twelve places Luke provides matching pairs of events, one involving a man and one a woman. Sometimes the paired events demonstrate that women and men are equal in their standing before God, are equally gifted, and are equally commissioned to serve. Sometimes they reveal women as the primary models for divine-human encounters, encounters which were impossible with the less faithful men around Jesus.

Recent writers have also pointed out that Luke's gospel begins and ends with special divine commissionings of women into ministry. God commissions a woman (Jesus' mother) prior to Jesus' birth (Lk. 1:26-38), and he commissions women subsequent to Jesus' resurrection (24:1-11). These commissionings stand parallel in form to all the major commissionings for ministry in Acts.

As already shown, John's gospel significantly highlights Jesus' interactions with women. The Samaritan woman to whom Jesus reveals his messianic and divine identity and who evangelizes her village, Mary who sits at Jesus' feet and anoints him for burial, Martha who responds to Jesus' word with a full confession of Christian faith, Mary Magdalene (apostle to the apostles) — all these stand as models for hearing the word of God and doing it. If leadership is a function of creative initiative and decisive action, the women who are depicted by John are well-qualified for the role.

The gospel writers do not ignore stories where men model faithful discipleship, but they seem to highlight those which feature women. It appears that the writers took affirmative action, attempting to bring a measure of balance in a world that favored men even more than ours does. However, the final goal is not to replace the male-oriented status quo with a feminist perspective. The final goal is to see humanity with the vision of Christ, a vision articulated so well by Paul in Galatians 3:28, "there is neither Jew nor Greek, slave nor free, male nor female, for you are all one in Christ Jesus." That is God's final will for his people, no matter how long it takes before the vision is fully realized.

THE REALISM OF JESUS

The New Testament does not hold out the hope that prior to God's final intervention to fully establish his kingdom, the will of God will ever be fully practiced on earth as it is in heaven. However, we must never forget that the mandate for Christian behavior is never "what people do." It is "what God calls them to do."

Jesus lived in the real world; and though he prepared the soil for the full implementation of his kingdom vision, he did not himself institute all the radical changes that the implementation of that vision would entail.

This is most clearly seen in Jesus' response to the Jew/Gentile question. His vision was clearly the establishment of a kingdom in which racial barriers would be eliminated, yet he limited his ministry almost exclusively to Jews. He strongly criticized Jewish religious leaders for their prejudice against and exclusion of Gentiles. He lessened the hold of Jewish ceremonial laws which held Gentiles at a distance. He even prepared the people for the abolition of Jewish food laws

(Mk. 7:19), but he did not directly evangelize Gentiles. In fact, God did not initiate the Gentile mission even at Pentecost. The destruction of Jew/Gentile barriers was part of the kingdom vision Jesus died to achieve. But it did not take effect right away. It happened within the developing history of the church (see Acts 10-15).

Nor did Jesus fully implement his vision for the abolition of social/economic discrimination. The abolition of slavery was not even contemplated as an agenda within first-century Christianity, but its eventual abolition was nonetheless an outcome of Christ's kingdom vision.

Jesus' vision for the abolition of sexual discrimination has also not been fully implemented. Some Bible students maintain that Jesus appointed only men to be his officially designated apostles because he intended to uphold a divinely ordained, role-differentiated, hierarchical "creation order," but a different explanation is more in keeping with Jesus' kingdom vision.

He did not appoint women for the same reason that he excluded Gentiles and slaves. The time was not ripe. The soil had not been sufficiently prepared. Just as Gentiles had to be "brought near through the blood of Christ" (Eph. 2:13) before they could be prepared for church ministries, so also women had to be called first to sit at Jesus' feet before they could be prepared for church ministries. Just as the church had to let Christ's kingdom vision re-shape many inherited racial prejudices before Gentiles could be fully incorporated into the church, so also the church must let Christ's kingdom vision re-shape many inherited sexual prejudices before women can be fully incorporated into church leadership.

THE CHALLENGE FOR TODAY

The challenge for today is to keep implementing the vision of Galatians 3:28. Several decades passed before the church understood that "neither Jew nor Greek" meant Jews and Greeks could be equal partners within the renewed humanity. Many centuries passed before the church understood that "neither slave nor free" meant that slavery could and should be abolished. We do not know how long it will take until the church understands that "neither male nor female" means that both genders are called equally to the ministries of the church.

The New Testament was not designed to establish limits in the implementation of the vision; it was designed to provide models and mandates for its continuing implementation. Implementing the kingdom vision for the abolition of racial discrimination in the church took place at different times and in different ways in Jerusalem and in Antioch.

Implementing the kingdom vision for the abolition of social/economic discrimination in the church also took place in different ways in the first-century churches of the Roman Empire and in the nineteenth-century churches of the American southern states.

We should not be surprised if implementing the kingdom vision for the abolition of sexual discrimination in the church takes place differently in the twentieth century than in the first, in predominately Muslim countries than in modern Europe or North America, and in rural communities than in urban settings.

Our world is diverse; our churches are diverse as well. While we sometimes struggle with disagreements and uncertainty, we must never lose sight of the radical principles Jesus so clearly instituted in his own ministry. If we practice these principles, we will certainly make progress in dealing with the sexual discrimination still existing in the church. If we practice these principles, the kingdom vision will become ever clearer and we will be able to see more clearly the implications for the ministry of women in the church.

SUGGESTIONS FOR READING

Brown, R.E. "Roles of Women in the Fourth Gospel." Blackfriars 52 (1971): 291- 299.

Evans, Mary E. Women in the Bible. InterVarsity, 1983.

Foh, Susan T. Women and the Word of God. Baker, 1979.

Malbon, E.S. "Fallible Followers: Women and Men in the Gospel of Mark." Semeia 28 (1983): 29-48.

Sayers, Dorothy. Are Women Human? InterVarsity, 1971.

Schneiders, S.M. "Women in the Fourth Gospel and the Role of Women in the Contemporary Church." Biblical Theology Bulletin 12 (1982): 35-45.

Raymond O. Bystrom

Galatians 3:28 and Pauline Practice

A little church in a remote area had been without a pastor for some time. Eventually, a daughter of the congregation, who had prepared for the ministry, came to serve the church as pastor. After seven years of ministry, she left for a larger church. Following her departure, a young man was invited to candidate for the vacant pastoral position by preaching a trial sermon. While the people were filing out of church after the service, a little girl was heard to say to her mother, "I didn't know that men could be pastors, too!"

This quieting, or disquieting, tale makes it sound as if it's no longer a man's world. The fact, however, is that most contemporary Christian congregations are in favor of keeping men dominant in church leadership roles. But is male dominance in church leadership and ministry really Christian?

Long ago, in a letter to the Christians of Galatia, Paul proclaimed that "in Christ Jesus" there is "neither . . . *male nor female*" (3:28). This is the most forthright statement in the New Testament on the equality of women with men before God. We read it and wish Paul had paused to explain it. But he offers no further comment at this point. Everyone, however, who takes God's Word seriously must ponder the meaning and implications of Paul's statement for congregational life. How is it related to the corporate life of the church? What implications does it have for women in ministry?

The crucial issue in this text in relation to the role of women in church leadership is whether equality in Christ refers to spiritual status before God only or also to ministerial function in the body of Christ.

YOU ARE ALL ONE IN CHRIST JESUS

Paul's "neither male nor female" is located at the conclusion of an argument about the sole condition for full inclusion in the Christian community (2:15—3:25). By faith in Christ Jesus both Jews and Gentiles are justified before God. By faith in Christ Jesus both Jews and Gentiles receive the promised Holy Spirit and are incorporated into Christ's community.

Beginning with 3:26 Paul spells out the consequences of his argument for the Galatian Christians by defining their status before God. He addresses them directly. The shift is from "we" to "you," from law to Christ, from exclusiveness to inclusiveness. Unity in Christ is the dominant motif: "You are all sons of God" and "you are all one in Christ Jesus." Jews and Gentiles together constitute the people of God. Jewish Christians no longer point to the law as the sign of their identity, but to Christ. All Christians, both Jewish and Gentile, belong to Christ.

To make sure there is no misunderstanding, Paul highlights several basic realities concerning the believers' status before God in Christ.

1. All believers are sons and daughters of God through faith and through incorporation into Christ's body (v. 26).

2. All believers are incorporated into Christ's body by personal faith in Christ. Baptism is the outward and visible sign of admission to God's new community (v. 27a).

3. All believers have undergone a spiritual transformation that makes them Christians. They have "clothed themselves with Christ" (v. 27b).

Then in three parallel statements in the present tense, Paul announces the consequences of "putting on Christ": "there is neither Jew nor Greek, slave nor free, male nor female." In the third couplet, Paul asserts that male and female have become one in Christ. The statement declares that this unity is already a reality in God's sight. Next Paul invites the Galatians to express this new reality in the church and in society through a new set of attitudes and reactions. When Jew and Greek, slave and free, male and female, have "clothed themselves with Christ," they are liberated from the divisions that separate them from one another.

Paul's statement here is widely regarded as the Magna Carta of the New Humanity because it defines, in a revolutionary manner, the nature of the Christian's new relationship of oneness with other believers in Christ's body. Ethnic, social and sexual relations have been turned upside down in Christ. Old distinctions, old divisions, old separations, have been canceled in Christ.

And since oneness in Christ is already a reality in the sight of God, Christians must seek to express their equality both inside and outside the church.

GREEK AND JEWISH THANKSGIVING FORMULA

The revolutionary nature of Paul's words in Galatians 3:28 can only be appreciated against the backdrop of the status of women in the ancient world. It is important to recall that Paul's threefold affirmation corresponds to both Jewish and Greek formulas where the distinctions are retained.

In the Greco-Roman world the status of women is reflected in the popular prayer of Greek men. They thanked the gods that they were born "a human being and not a beast, next a man and not a woman, thirdly, a Greek and not a barbarian." Admittedly, Greek literature often affirms the equality of women and men in principle, but Greek society rarely achieved it in practice.

In Jewish circles a similar thanksgiving formula was commonly used. At the beginning of morning prayers, the male Jew prayed: "Blessed be God that he did not make me a Gentile; blessed be God that he did not make me an ignorant peasant or slave; blessed be God that he did not make me a woman."

The reason for this threefold thanksgiving by male Jews was not blatant demeaning of Gentiles, slaves, or women, but rather that these persons were restricted from many religious privileges open to free Jewish males. For example, a screen separated women from men in the synagogues, symbolizing woman's restricted role. Indeed, women were not normally allowed to participate in the actual service. Also, the study of the Law was off-limits for women. A married woman's role was essentially limited to homemaking. While exceptions can be cited, nowhere in ancient Judaism was any real effort made to practice, or even to propose, the social and religious equality of the sexes.

In contrast to such statements that accent male superiority, Paul writes that in Christ "there is neither Jew nor Greek, slave nor free, male nor female." Quite likely Paul himself was raised to thank God that he was not born a Gentile, a slave, or a woman. If so, he knew that Galatians 3:28 deliberately contradicted each phrase of his former prayer. Yet he unabashedly announces that in God's sight and in God's community national, social, and sexual privileges are abolished, "for you are all one in Christ Jesus."

BAPTISMAL CONFESSION
OF THE EARLY CHURCH

Some of Paul's interpreters maintain that we should not over-emphasize the third couplet of Galatians 3:28 ("neither . . . male nor female"). After all, there are no parallels to it elsewhere in the New Testament. Jesus himself never said anything quite so explicit about the equality of the sexes. Hence, these interpreters argue that these words were merely a peculiar idea of Paul's, not shared by others in the early church.

It is significant that in the larger passage under discussion (Gal. 3:26-29), we find Paul's only explicit reference to baptism in the entire letter. Galatians 3:28 is part of an early Christian baptismal confession. Both the structure and the content of the entire passage indicate that these verses contain a fragment of a baptismal confession of the early church that Paul uses to support his argument in Galatians 3:1-25. One can leap-frog from verse 26 to verse 29, omitting verses 27-28, without sensing any break in Paul's logic or grammar.

It is also significant that the last clause of verse 28 ("for you are all one in Christ Jesus") clearly parallels verse 26 ("for you are all sons of God through faith in Christ Jesus"), except for the Pauline phrase "through faith." Thus, the "for" of verse 27 introduces an explanatory statement in support of the affirmation of verse 26. In other words, Paul is quoting verses 27-28 to undergird his argument.

Note that only the first couplet in verse 28 ("there is neither Jew nor Greek") is directly related to Paul's argument in Galatians. Paul has not mentioned the relation of the sexes in arguing with the Judaizers at Galatia. Yet in these verses he makes the strange statement that in Christ there is "neither . . . male nor female."

Notice too that the pairings of Galatians 3:28 are found elsewhere in Paul's letters. "For we were all baptized by one Spirit into one body—whether Jews or Greeks, slaves or free—and we were all given the one Spirit to drink" (1 Cor. 12:13). "Here there is no Greek or Jew, circumcised or uncircumcised, barbarian, Scythian, slave or free, but Christ is all, and is in all" (Col. 3:11).

The pairings occur in either abbreviated (Corinthians) or expanded forms (Colossians) but in the same order (cf. 1 Cor. 7:17-20, 21-24, 25-28), suggesting a degree of fixity in Paul's mind. Furthermore, the pairings of Galatians 3:28 and 1 Corinthians 12:13 appear explicitly in connection with baptism and those of Colossians 3:11 are indirectly associated with baptism

(2:12; 3:9-10). Yet baptism as a subject is not being discussed in either passage.

All of this suggests that these pairings were originally formulated in a baptismal setting in the early church. At some point in the baptismal ceremony, perhaps as the newly-baptized Christians were extended the right-hand of fellowship, an elder informed them of their status as "sons and daughters of God through faith in Jesus Christ." Then he explained how their oneness in Christ made the difference between Jew and Greek, slave and free, male and female, irrelevant before God. In this way, the early Christians celebrated in their baptismal ceremony the marvelous truth that in Christ Jesus the old racial, social, and sexual divisions had been healed.

When first-century Christians spoke of being "sons and daughters of God," "baptized into Christ," and "clothed with Christ" (3:26-27) they simultaneously spoke of their faith in terms of a new social dynamic within the faith community in which there was "neither Jew nor Greek, slave nor free, male nor female." They saw that the gospel called them to treat all people impartially and to express in daily life those attitudes and actions that would eliminate barriers of prejudice and inequality.

In short, Paul has "lifted" Galatians 3:27-28 from a baptismal liturgy of the early church and used it to remind the Galatians of words they had undoubtedly heard before in the context of their own baptism and incorporation into the church. Indeed, on the occasion of their baptism they agreed to live with one another in community on the basis of their oneness in Christ. They were now being reminded by Paul that in the redemption provided through Christ, God had eliminated the divisions and inequalities between Jew and Greek, slave and free, male and female. Thus, Paul asks the Galatians, and by extension, the twentieth-century church, "where is the evidence of your equality in Christ in your corporate life?"

SEXUAL UNITY OR UNIFORMITY IN CHRIST?

After Paul states that "there is neither . . . male nor female," he speaks of the fact that all who are in Christ are "one." What sort of oneness or unity does Paul contemplate? What kind of inequality is abolished in Christ?

Although the three groupings Paul mentions are not exactly parallel in construction, they are to be interpreted in the same way. There is a change of construction in the third couplet. Most versions retain the "neither . . . male nor female" translation for the sake of symmetry. Literally, however, Paul says: "no male and female." The change is a reflection of the language of the Greek translation of Genesis 1:27. However, the change in construction does not change the meaning of the third couplet in the series. Paul makes no distinction between the three pairings.

So what happens to the racial, social, and sexual differences between people? Paul does not mean that the differences between race, rank, and sex no longer exist in Christ. If Paul himself is taken as a model, one must say that the differences between the categories remain. Paul continues to reflect a Jewish identity and self-awareness (Gal. 2:15; 2 Cor. 11:22; Phil. 3:5; Rom. 11:14), to treat Jews and Gentiles as distinct ethnic units (Rom. 9-11), to address slaves, slave-owners, men and women, as distinct groups. Therefore, the unity which he declares is not one in which ethnic, social, and sexual distinctions disappear. Rather, it is a unity in which the barriers and hostility between the three categories are destroyed. Unity does not require uniformity; male and female remain what they are. Sexually specific differences are not denied for the sake of some abstract equality. Indeed, Paul himself is not really concerned with such abstractions; he is concerned with the practical and everyday affairs of church life in which men and women, like Jews and Gentiles, slaves and free persons, are here and now sons and daughters in God's community.

SPIRITUAL AND SOCIAL UNITY IN CHRIST

In the history of the Christian church there has been a tendency to limit the degree to which "there is no male and female." Many Christians have framed the new reality and the new relations of Galatians 3:28 only in spiritual terms. For example, it has been argued that the words "no male and female" relate only to the common way men and women join the Christian community through baptism.

There is little doubt that in all three pairings of Galatians 3:28 Paul thought first in terms of the relationship between God and humanity. When it comes to the grounds of entry into the Christian community, all are on equal footing before God. Fellowship between God and humanity is no longer limited along national, social, or sexual lines.

But Paul's proclamation is a message of equality that has both spiritual and social dimensions. Indeed it speaks with meaning to all three areas of life where the Gospel had a particular social impact on first-century Christians—national, social, and sexual.

Paul speaks without qualification or reservations in Galatians 3:28. He asserts that sexual differences that divide and alienate male and female are suspended. They are both nullified as conditions for salvation and as social barriers between human beings. Not only are religious advantages before God based on sexual distinctions eliminated, but sexually determined religious roles within the Christian community are also broken. Male dominance and preference is at an end.

Thus, when spelling out the new relationships which are meant by God to exist in the church, Paul explicitly says that in the same way that Jews are to have no exclusive privileges over Gentiles and free persons to have no exclusive advantages over slaves, so men are to have no exclusive prerogatives over women.

According to the gospel which had seized the life and mind of Paul, the status of Gentiles, slaves, and women has been equalized with that of Jews, masters and males within the Christian community. For Paul, all three groups have equal standing before God spiritually and within the church socially when "in Christ." It is evident from Paul's confrontation with Peter at Antioch (Gal. 2:11-21) that Paul saw the social implications of the equalizing of Jew and Gentile in Christ. Paul did not say that Jews and Greeks are one in personal salvation, but that in other respects, such as eating at social gatherings, things remain as they always have been with Jews eating separately. To the contrary, he defended the right of Gentiles to be present with Jews at social gatherings and on an equal basis. He insisted on complete social equality, for he believed that the new unity in Christ is intended to shape the new life in the church.

It is also evident from Paul's dealing with Onesimus, the runaway slave, that he had begun to grapple with the social implications of the equalizing of slave and free person in Christ. Paul reluctantly returns Onesimus, who has become a Christian, to his master Philemon. Although Paul politely hints to Philemon that he should set his slave free ("I could be bold and order you to do what you ought to do," v. 8), he did not confront Philemon on the slave issue like he did Peter on the issue of Jews and Gentiles eating together. Instead, he appeals to Philemon by writing a moving letter on the equality that binds all persons who have been clothed in Christ. Onesimus is "no longer a slave, but better than a slave, a dear brother." Within the organic unity of the church, slaves and owners are now brothers. Philemon is to welcome Onesimus as if he were the apostle Paul himself (v. 17). Thus, in his dealings with Onesimus, Paul provides us with important clues to what the practice of the Christian community ought to be on the slave/free person distinction.

In short, if the Jew/Gentile and slave/free person distinction is considered irrelevant within the church, then the male/female distinction should also be considered irrelevant.

PAUL'S APPLICATION OF SEXUAL EQUALITY IN CHRIST

Paul's talk about sexual equality in Christ did not simply remain a theory. Women played a significant role in Paul's churches. He acted out the gospel principle of sexual equality in Christ in a remarkable way for a former rabbi.

Paul's greetings to his fellow workers in Romans 16 indicates something of his attitude toward women in the church. The apostle greets by name no fewer than six women, and all six are spoken of as having participated in some form of Christian ministry. (See also Chapters 2, 10, 13.)

He begins the chapter by commending Phoebe (vv. 1-2), who is described as "our sister," that is, a member of the Christian community. Also, she is called both a deacon (*diakonos*) and a helper/patron (*prostatis*). The word *diakonos* was an official title of church leadership. It is used in 1 Corinthians 3:5 and 2 Corinthians 3:6, 6:4, 11:15, and 23 to refer to missionaries, including Paul himself. A deacon was a missionary entrusted with preaching and tending churches. Phoebe clearly functioned as a leader of the local churches in Cenchreae. The second title associated with Phoebe confirms this impression. She was also a "protectoress," or "patroness." Recent research has shown that patronesses were persons of high social standing and means with a house large enough for the church to gather. Such women were responsible for the ordering of the congregation in their home and presiding over the celebration of the Lord's Supper. Phoebe was such a significant person that Paul instructed the Roman churches "to receive her in the Lord as befits the saints, and help her in whatever she may require from you." Such hosting instructions are common in ancient literature. They ask people to "roll out the red carpet" for important people. In other words, Phoebe is to be received with the honor appropriate to her position as a congregational leader.

After his commendation of Phoebe, Paul greets a number of persons by name. Five are women, and all five are spoken of as having participated in Christian ministry. Prisca, or Priscilla, together with her husband Aquila, is greeted first and identified as Paul's "fellow workers in Christ Jesus." In the New Testament

Prisca's name is more often than not placed before her husband's. Perhaps she came from a higher social class (a Jewess with Roman citizenship) than her husband or maybe she was a more prominent worker in the church.

In addition to Prisca, Paul greets Mary, Tryphena, Tryphosa and Persis. Each woman is commended for having worked hard in the Lord. The emphasis on working is characteristic of Paul's remarks about each woman whom he greets.

Paul considered women to be full members of the Christian community. He does not speak of women in a condescending or patronizing fashion. Indeed, one gets the impression that he happily worked side by side with a number of women in his various missionary travels and saw them as partners and not subordinates.

Further evidence of Paul's practice of the principle of no male and female in Christ may be seen in his appreciation of the Philippian women who labored side by side with him in the gospel (Phil. 4:2-3). Euodia and Syntyche are described as "women who have contended at my side in the cause of the gospel, along with Clement and the rest of my fellow workers, whose names are in the book of life." Quite likely we will never know what these women actually did to merit Paul's commendation. But it is self-evident from these references that women worked alongside men in the Pauline churches and did so with Paul's unqualified approval.

As one student of Paul explains, "No more restriction is implied in Paul's equalizing of the status of male and female in Christ than in his equalizing of the status of Jew and Gentile, or slave and free person. . . . If a Gentile may exercise spiritual leadership in church as freely as a Jew, or a slave as freely as a citizen, why not a woman as freely as a man?"

IMPLICATIONS FOR THE CHRISTIAN COMMUNITY TODAY

Paul deserves an accolade for his efforts to apply the gospel principles of freedom and equality to the situations of his day. He set a pattern and marked out a path for subsequent Christian generations to follow both in thought and action.

No one doubts that the lifestyle of the church must be consistent with the gospel of the church. Proclamation must lead to demonstration of the gospel principles in the here and now. And since Paul intends his message of male and female equality in Christ to be understood both spiritually and socially, how can we welcome women to the ministry but restrict their functions? Isn't the issue one of either keeping women from the ministry entirely or opening all its functions to them?

SUGGESTIONS FOR READING

Betz, H.D. Galatians: A Commentary on Paul's Letter to the Churches in Galatia. Fortress, 1979.

Bruce, F.F. Commentary on Galatians. NIGTC. Eerdmans, 1982.

Hurley, J.B. Man and Woman in Biblical Perspective. Academie Books, 1981.

Longenecker, R.N. New Testament Social Ethics for Today. Eerdmans, 1984.

Snodgrass, K. "Galatians 3:28 — Connundrum or Solution?" Women, Authority and the Bible. A. Michelsen, ed. InterVarsity Press, 1986: 161-180.

Terrien, S. Till the Heart Sings: A Biblical Theology of Manhood and Womanhood. Fortress, 1985: 159-174.

Witherington, B. "Rite and Rights for Women." New Testament Studies 27 (1981): 593-604.

COVERED AND QUIET? 8

Katrina Poetker

Women in the Corinthian Church:
1 Corinthians 11:2-16; 14:34-36

A young woman stood at the back of the church with a child, trying to keep her quiet while listening to the service. She and her husband had driven 50 miles to bring a mission message in a rural church. As she quieted her daughter, the outside door opened and a family walked in. They were late, but what made them stand out among the other worshipers was that the mother wore a piece of cloth on her head, covering her hair—a rare practice in the churches of the area.

Following the service, the two couples struck up a conversation. "I'm interested in your head covering," the missionary said. "What does it mean to you?" The woman proceeded to explain that she had recently started to wear it after being convinced that this was the true meaning of 1 Corinthians 11.

*"Does it also signify an authority structure placing you
under your husband?" she was asked. "Yes, it does,"
she answered smiling.*

Most of us can accept a woman's choice to wear a
headcovering. In fact, it wasn't too many years ago that
nearly all women wore hats on Sunday morning — more
as a matter of fashion, perhaps, than as a sign of authority. But while we are comfortable with a woman's
choice to wear a headcovering (something our churches
do not regularly practice), we are not as comfortable
with some women's desire to publicly minister in the
church.

Are there God-ordained levels of authority which do
not permit female leadership in the church? Two passages which bear careful study are 1 Corinthians 11:2-
16 and 14:34-36. They are most often used to place restrictions on women, but a close study of the passages
may indicate a wider acceptance of women in public
ministry.

THE CONTEXT

In 1 Corinthians 7:1-16:12 Paul responds to issues
raised in a letter from the churches of Corinth. Chapter
7 discusses questions about marriage, Chapters 8—9
problems of meat offered to idols, and Chapters 11—14
problems in Christian worship. The last section,
Chapters 11—14, address two problems in an ABA parallel structure:

A. Prayer and prophecy, 11:2-16
    B. The Lord's Supper, 11:17-34
A. Prayer and prophecy, 12:1—14:40.

The context is clearly the public gatherings of the Christian community. The first text unit and one of the last concern the role of women in these gatherings.

LET HER HEAD BE COVERED (1 Cor. 11:2-16)

The text in 1 Corinthians 11 is a discussion about men and women praying and prophesying, about their heads, and about the covering of their heads. The passage is difficult because we no longer understand some of the terms and the customs referred too.

For example, we do not really know what Paul meant when he referred to the covering of the head while praying and prophesying in Corinth. It may be that Paul was referring to some sort of external head-covering. Jewish women appeared in public only with their heads covered. The evidence for Greek women is less certain. Greek religious practices of that time included cultic drunkenness, sexual license and improper dress, all problems which spilled over into the Corinthian church. Sex reversal (wearing the clothing or hairstyle of the opposite sex) also took place. An uncovered or a shaven head for a woman or long hair for a man was considered a sexual inversion. In places where a headcovering was worn, it served as a symbol of female identity.

Or, Paul may have been referring to a hairstyle, recommending that hair be bound instead of worn in free-flowing style. In a Jewish context free-flowing hair was a sign of sexual availability and infidelity. In pagan settings it may have had the same meaning, but it was also associated with the ecstatic female worship of oriental gods. Wearing the hair on the head symbolized marital faithfulness and dignity in worship.

Given these options, what did the exhortation about headcoverings for women in public worship mean for the Corinthian Christians? A closer look at our text helps us sort out these possibilities.

The text is structured on an ABA pattern:

A. Sexual distinctions are rooted in creation and Christian worship must reflect them (vv. 3-10)

   B. Sexual equality is rooted in redemption, and creation seen in its light, but sexual distinctions are not transcended (vv. 11-12)

A. Sexual distinctions are rooted in the nature of things and Christian worship must reflect this (vv. 13-15)

Covering the Head

The passage begins with three references to "head" in verse 3. Some have understood this verse to outline a structure of authority, a "chain of command," but this is unlikely.

The Greek word *kephale*, translated as "head," most frequently means "source" or "origin." A secondary meaning is "chief" or "person of authority," but this meaning is rarely used. The creation references and the context of the passage stress relatedness rather than an order of authority.

The passage is a commentary on Genesis 2: "The head of every man is Christ, the head of woman is the man, and the head of Christ is God." The theological basis for the statement is given later in verse 8: "man is not made from woman, but woman from man." The reference is the creation of woman from man, i.e., the rib (Gen. 2:21-22). The "head" here clearly refers to source. In the ancient world origin determined purpose.

Therefore, Paul goes on to say later, "neither was man created for woman, but woman for man."

The three phrases also are in the wrong order to convey a structure of authority. A logical approach for expressing authority would have begun with God, followed by Christ, man, and finally woman. Gilbert Bilezikian points out that the order here expresses a **chronological sequence** in which Christ was the source of life at creation (Col. 1:16), woman was created from man (Gen. 2), and God was the source of Christ's life. The emphasis is on relatedness, not authority.

We can discern from Paul's letter that after becoming Christians, the Corinthians began to view the distinctions between male and female as no longer important because they had already become as the angels and were thus beyond human sexuality. To combat this misperception, Paul argues for the importance of holiness and faithfulness in all aspects of life, including the physical (1 Cor. 7 argues this for marriage, Ch. 11 for the importance of sexual differentiation, and Ch. 15 for the reality of a bodily resurrection). The significance of the "headcovering" is its affirmation of distinctive sexual identity.

A further clue to this understanding is Paul's use of the word "shame." The word carries a sense of public disgrace, of humiliation in front of others. Paul uses the same word in 11:22 to say that the poor were being humiliated at the Lord's Supper. It seems clear from his writing that the covering and uncovering of men's and women's heads delivered a message of shame to the surrounding culture. The believer's behavior had the potential to bring shame to the church and the gospel by associating the church with the pagan practices mentioned earlier. The headcovering was a matter of retaining sexual identity and commitment to marriage.

Praying and Prophesying

Paul's reference to women praying and prophesying (v. 5) means women participated in and led corporate worship. In the Old Testament, prophecy was the reception and declaration of divine revelation. The significance of the prophetic function is similar in the New Testament. The purpose of prophecy, whether by men or women, is the strengthening, encouragement, and comfort of the people. It is a gift which edifies the church (14:3-4).

Women such as Miriam and Deborah shared the prophetic gift with men in the Old Testament (see Ch. 3). Similarly, women participated in the outpouring of the Spirit at Pentecost, spoke in tongues, and received the gift of prophecy (Acts 1:14; 2:1-4, 17-21). In the chapters concerning spiritual gifts there is no indication that certain gifts are restricted to men (Rom. 12, 1 Cor. 12—14). All the gifts are given as the Spirit wills. In fact, Paul's list of the spiritual gifts indicates that prophecy is one of the three higher gifts, and is to be desired more than the other gifts (1 Cor. 12:28-31; 14:1).

Creation and Glory

Paul provides a framework for interpreting the practice of headcovering in verses 7-12. He places corresponding thoughts in reverse sequence to each other. Verses 7-9 form the first part, verse 10 the center of the pattern, and then verses 11 and 12 correspond to 8 and 9 in reverse order. The following illustrates this relationship:

A. Source of creation (v. 8)
   B. Relationship in creation (v. 9)
      C. Authority (v. 10)
   B. Relationship in the Lord (v. 11)
A. Source in God (v. 12).

The reason a woman should wear a headcovering, and the man should not is that "the man is the image and glory of God" and "woman is the glory of man" (v. 7). Paul describes man as "the image and glory of God." He does not say that woman is not the image of God. That would contradict Genesis 1:27. What Paul says is that she is man's glory. How should we understand this phrase?

The word "glory" can refer to brightness and splendor, but also to fame, honor, and a good reputation. The latter use provides a direct contrast to the "shame" mentioned in verses 4-6. "Glory" means that the existence of one brings glory and honor to the other. Remember Adam's response in Genesis 2 when he saw Eve for the first time? He "gloried" in her.

Paul goes on to explain this understanding of glory in verses 8-9 by referring to Genesis 1:26-27 and 2:18-23. He emphasizes the differentness of the sexes in creation. In Genesis 2 woman is formed from the body of a man and for the sake of the man, confirming the "source" meaning of "head" in verse 3. He is her origin. She is his glory in that her existence brings honor and praise to the man. The man is not, however, her maker. The formation of woman from man does not imply an authority structure any more than man's formation from the dust implies his subordination to the earth. Instead, woman is the completion of God's creation, the perfect partner for man. She is his glory.

Creation differentiates the sexes. Men and women are different because of the design of the Creator. "On account of this," Paul states in verse 10, "a woman is obligated to have authority upon the head." The meaning of "authority" (*exousia*) is a central issue in the passage. One translation states that the woman should have a "sign of authority" on her head to indicate that she is under the authority of man. But the text, translated very literally above, does not say that. Furthermore, nowhere in the New Testament or Greek literature does the form of the word here mean that one should be under the authority of another. "Authority" carries its normal sense—the woman's right to choose.

But what does the woman have authority over? The text says that the woman ought to have authority over her head. She has authority over her physical head, meaning that she can do as she wishes in regard to headcovering. This is supported by verse 13, where Paul appeals to the Corinthians to judge for themselves on this matter. Similarly, in Chapter 9 Paul uses the same word (authority) when he writes about his right to have support from the church, even though he did not use this authority (9:12, 19-23). In the same way, Paul states that a woman has authority over her head, but that authority should be used in the best interests of the church and the gospel. In the Corinthian situation, this meant that she should cover her head. Women should wear a headcovering as a sign of their femaleness. To wear a headcovering meant to accept one's created sexuality.

The concluding phrase in verse 10, "because of the angels," is puzzling. Many interpretations have been offered but a definite conclusion is impossible. Apparently there was a common understanding between Paul and the Corinthians which he leaves unspoken.

Woman and Man in Christ

In verses 11 and 12 Paul points to the principle of interdependence. Neither women nor men are independent of each other. Paul's phrase, "in the Lord," is very important. Paul contrasts the relationship of men and women in creation with that of the new creation. In creation woman was created from man. In the Lord, however, there is a new relation between men and women. They are mutually interdependent as Galatians 3:28 states. Sexual distinctions remain, but men and women are equal in redemption. Men and women are both different and equal. Created differences and redemptive equality are divine gifts. Therefore, creation is not canceled out by redemption. These two verses can be seen as the climax of this section, pointing towards the way women and men relate to each other in God's kingdom.

Two More Arguments

Paul returns to his original concern regarding women covering their heads at the close of the passage, vv. 13-16. He uses two arguments to support the practice. First, sexual distinctions are rooted in nature. "Nature" teaches the appropriateness of a headcovering (vv. 14-15). Certain things were symbols of femaleness and maleness in Paul's world. They distinguished the sexes. Among the signs of femaleness was long hair.

Paul's second argument is the practice in other churches (v. 16). Women kept their heads covered during worship in the Pauline churches to affirm their female sexuality. For the Corinthian women to remove the headcovering would signify disagreement with the larger church.

Summary

The problem Paul addresses in Chapter 11 is that some Corinthian women were praying and prophesying in public worship without headcoverings. Paul rejects any female participation in community worship which did not involve the wearing of a headcovering. He grounds his stance in three arguments: (1) creation differentiates the sexes; (2) nature differentiates the sexes; (3) the practice in the Pauline churches differentiates the sexes.

The theological issue, as Paul defines it, is whether redemption (salvation and freedom in Christ) cancels out creation (human sexuality), or whether creation and redemption are not interdependent. Some Corinthian women acted as though redemption freed them from their created sexuality.

Throughout the passage Paul stresses the relatedness of man and woman, and the implications of this for participation in corporate worship. Paul argues that redemption (Christian equality) enhances creation (sexual differentiation). He wants women to cover their heads when praying or prophesying in order to correct those who claimed that women had gone beyond sexual identity. The headcovering was to symbolize their sexual identity as women and their faithfulness to their marriages.

Paul also describes the creation of woman from and for man—the completion of man in woman. While women have authority to choose their own headcovering, in the Lord women and men were to exercise mutual cooperation and interdependence.

Paul does not aim to silence women in Christian worship in Chapter 11 or to subordinate them to men, but to guarantee that their worship roles and leadership gives expression to who they are as women.

LET HER BE SILENT (1 Cor. 14:34-35)

The second passage, 1 Corinthians 14:34-35, seems to contradict 1 Corinthians 11:5. These verses appear to contend for the complete silence of women in the church.

Verses 34-35 can be interpreted in a number of ways. Some see them as a further restriction to 11:2-16 on women speaking in church. Others maintain that these verses were not written by Paul but were a later scribal addition since one group of ancient manuscripts place verses 34-35 at the end of the chapter. A third interpretation argues that the verses are a quotation from the opposition, or a restatement of the Corinthians' view, perhaps of one party within the church. (V. 36 begins with a small Greek word which is usually left untranslated in our English Bibles. This word can mean "what," indicating that the negative questions which follow refute the preceding sentences. In this interpretation Paul answers the opposition in v. 36 by saying "What! Did the word of God originate with you, or are you the only one it has reached?" The content of vv. 34 and 35 is then emphatically denied by Paul in v. 36.) Finally, the verses can be read in their larger context—a series of instructions regarding behavior in public meetings (1 Cor. 14:26-40). The following interpretation is based on the assumption that Paul wrote these words, that they form part of his general instructions, and that they do not contradict Chapter 11.

Instructions for Worship

Paul gives a series of general instructions in verses 26-40 with three specific instructions concerning tongues (vv. 27-28), prophecy (vv. 29-33), and married women in the congregation (vv. 34-36). Each of these instructions is similar, addressing a situation in the Corinthians' public meetings. Paul's main concern is orderly behavior during their meetings. His reason for these directives is to show that God is not a God of disorder but of peace, as in all the churches of the saints (v. 33).

To better understand this passage, we need to determine the meaning of three important words in the following phrases: "Let them be *silent*," "let them be *subject*," and "to *speak*."

The Greek word translated "silent" is found twice in verses 28 and 30. It does not refer to absolute silence, or non-participation, but to self-control. Again, Paul's chief concern is the orderly, Spirit-led behavior of men and women in worship gatherings.

The Greek word for "subject" may mean to be identified with, to come under the influence of, or to be joined to something or someone. The form in which it appears indicates that the person is to control him or herself. A similar meaning of the word is found in verse 32, where the prophets are to "control" their own spirits. A literal translation would read, "let them control themselves, as the law also says."

The word "speak" can refer to uncontrolled, disruptive speech. Verse 35 implies that the problem addressed was married women asking questions during the meeting. Paul encouraged them to ask their husbands at home instead of during the meeting. It is interesting to note the important contrast these verses provide to the common understanding of marriage at the time. The Corinthian Christians lived in a culture in which husbands and wives seldom conversed or spent time together. Clearly, the relationship between Christian spouses was to be more intimate.

What Were the Women Doing?

Again, just as in Paul's instructions about head-coverings, we cannot be sure of the precise situation. Was Paul restricting some kind of inspired speech other than prophecy, perhaps tongues itself? Nothing in the letter indicates such a restriction. Were women disrupting the church's meetings with some form of ecstatic behavior and speech, or by asking their husbands questions from across the room? This seems more likely considering the surrounding Greek religious practices and the exhortation to ask questions at home.

It is also unclear precisely which law they were breaking. Nowhere else does Paul refer to "law" in the way he does here. There is no law prohibiting women from speaking in the Old Testament, not even in rabbinic interpretation. "The law" probably refers to Greek and Roman civil laws which had been established to curb the cultic excesses of women. The reference then reinforces Paul's concern that the behavior of the Corinthian women should be above reproach.

CONCLUSION

The two Corinthian passages we have studied provide significant insights for questions regarding the role of women in the church. Chapter 11 clearly indicates that Paul recognized women's involvement and leadership in the church as women. His only concern is that women be women, that they retain their sexual identity in leadership. Both texts teach the importance of maintaining distinctions between men and women. The passages teach the compatibility and mutual interdependence of men and women in God's kingdom, and emphasize the importance of maintaining family and marriage commitments while involved in Christian worship.

SUGGESTIONS FOR READING

Bilezikian, Gilbert. Beyond Sex Roles. Baker, 1985.

Fee, Gordon D. The First Epistle to the Corinthians. Eerdmans, 1987.

Fiorenza, Elizabeth Schluesser. In Memory of Her. Crossroads, 1984.

Flanagan, Neal M. and Snyder, Edwin Hunter. "Did Paul Put Down Women in 1 Cor. 14.34-36? " Biblical Theology Bulletin 11 (1981): 10-12.

Kroeger, Richard, and Kroeger, Catherine Clark. "Pandemonium and Silence at Corinth." Reformed Journal 28 (1978): 6-11.

_____. "Sexual Identity in Corinth: Paul Faces a Crisis." Reformed Journal 28 (1978): 11-15.

Mercadante, Linda. "From Hierarchy to Equality: A Comparison of Past and Present Interpretations of 1 Cor. 11.2-16 in Relation to the Changing Status of Women in Society." Master of Christian Studies Thesis. Regent College, Vancouver, 1978.

Michelson, Alvera, ed. <u>Women, Authority and the Bible</u>.
    InterVarsity, 1986.

Odell-Scott, David W. "Let the Women Speak in Church: an
    Egalitarian Interpretation of 1 Corinthians 14.33b-36."
    <u>Biblical Theology Bulletin</u> 13 (1983): 90-93.

Talbert, Charles H. <u>Reading Corinthians</u>. Crossroad, 1987.

THE HUSBAND IS THE HEAD OF THE WIFE 9

John E. Toews

The Husband and Wife Relation: Ephesians 5:21-33

Several passages were read rather regularly in family devotions. Ephesians 5:21-33 was one of them. As the boys in the family grew older they recognized that the marital model of their parents was a democratic one. They began to wonder what happened when their parents could not reach consensus. Finally one of the boys asked the parents. "Well," the mother replied, "I don't recall that the issue has ever really come up." "Oh yes it has," the father said. "You remember the time we couldn't agree and I had to break the tie?"

The father explained to the boys how these things work among well-married Christian people. The normal rhythm of marriage, he observed, is one of full equality and mutual submission. "We submit to each other; it's a sign that we have the Spirit of Christ." In some areas the husband submits to the wife's superiority of judgment and expertise, and in others she submits to his. Neither worries that the other will take advantage.

But then one day a real disagreement arises. Each tries to submit to the other. So the husband says, "Dear, we'll do it your way." "Oh no," she responds, "you're right and we'll follow your lead." They are deadlocked. Finally, the husband stands up to his full height, and says. "Look, for once in our marriage I'm going to have to invoke the headship principle and break the tie. You are right, we're going to do it your way, and I don't want to hear another word about it."

"That's the kind of tie I had to break once," the father concluded.

Why a study of Ephesians 5:21-33 in a book on women in ministry? The text concerns the relationship between husband and wife in the family. It does not speak to questions of church leadership.

This passage is studied for two reasons. First, it says the husband is the head of the wife. This "headship" language is often read to mean that women are inferior and subservient. And this interpretation then has been applied to women in the church; women are to be subordinate to men in the church. Secondly, evangelicals are divided on how to understand this text. Does the text advocate equal or unequal relationships in marriage?

TWO VIEWS

View One: Women Are to Be Subordinate

Evangelical theologians S.B. Clark and J.B. Hurley state that this text teaches hierarchical relationships. Its focus is the order between husband and wife. The wife is to submit to her husband. The text does not teach mutual submission, they argue. Only one person is exhorted to subordination, and that person is the wife. The phrase "to one another" means to the superior person and not mutually. This subordination involves the obedience of the wife to the husband "in everything," meaning in every area of the wife's life. The purpose of her subordination is unity in the family, as between Christ and the church.

The wife's exhortation to submission is framed by "because you fear Christ" (v. 21) and "as to the Lord" (v. 22). The teaching is not based on human authority, but has the authority of the Lord. "The fear of Christ" corresponds to the "fear of God" in the Old Testament. It is a fear that produces obedience and an attitude of submission. The wife's relation to Christ shapes her subordination to her husband. She should act toward her husband as she would to Christ. The husband has authority over his wife because Christ delegated it. When the wife submits to her husband, she is obeying Christ.

The husband is exhorted to love his wife with a "service-love" like Christ has for the church. This love makes her subordination easier.

The exhortation to submission is grounded in the head/body relationship. The husband is the head of the wife. "Headship" means a governing and representative function. The wife must be completely under the authority of her husband.

View Two: Mutual Submission

Wheaton College's Gilbert Bilezikian offers a quite different interpretation. The point of the text is mutual submission. Submission is defined by "to one another." The qualification rules out hierarchical relations, for to be "subject to one another" is only possible among equals. Subjection is a vertical relation between ruler and subject, but mutual submission is a horizontal relation between equals.

The instruction to the wife is introduced by the exhortation to mutual submission in verse 21. Verse 22 does not have a verb, and so is nonsensical if the meaning of verse 21 does not control it. The entire passage concludes with a quotation from Genesis 2:24 (vv. 31-32), which speaks about the husband and wife becoming one flesh. Furthermore, because Christ is the model of mutual submission, "as to the Lord" means the wife is to commit herself to her husband in the same way she commits herself to Christ. Her devotion and loving service to Christ and to her husband have the same quality.

"Headship" in this interpretation means source, not ruler. The husband is the source of the wife's life, not her ruler. Therefore, the wife is never commanded to obey the husband, and the husband is never commanded to exercise authority over his wife.

The husband is to love the wife. The demands on the husband are more stringent and exhaustive than on the wife. It is impossible to love without submitting. The nature of the husband's loving submission is defined by the example of Christ as servant on the cross.

Is a Resolution Possible?

The two interpretations highlight the issue. What is the meaning of "headship" and "submission" language? Does the text teach that husbands are over their wives or that both are equal? Are wives to submit to husbands, or are wives and husbands mutually submissive to each other?

THE LANGUAGE OF EPHESIANS 5:21-33

The two critical terms in the text are "headship" and "submission." "Headship" (*kephale*) has two possible meanings. First, as a biological term, it denotes source or origin. Secondly, as a political word it means authority or leader. It can mean either. Therefore, the meaning of the word in any given text is determined by the context. Most scholars agree that in 1 Corinthians 11 "headship" means "source" or "origin" (see Ch. 8). The creation account states that woman was created from man, man was born from woman. Man as the head of woman means he is the source of her life just as she is the source of his life. Headship in 1 Corinthians 11 is not a power term, but a descriptive word denoting origin or source.

The context in Ephesians must also determine the meaning of headship. The term is used in three texts: 1:22, 4:15 and 5:23. In 1:22 Christ is made the head of all things for the church. Christ is made the prime minister (to sit at the right hand means to be made the prime minister in the ancient world) of the cosmos for the church. Headship is a power or authority term here. Christians grow into Christ as the head (4:15). Christ as the prime minister expresses his rule in the world by distributing gifts. Church leaders are to enable the many and different gifts to function in unity. The purpose is to build up the body of Christ to the fullness of Christ. Headship again is leader language, and thus a power term. In 5:23 the husband is defined as the head of the wife. Most "traditional" interpreters read "head" as a power term here. "Liberationist" interpreters read it as source language. I see it as a political word that means power or authority because of its other uses in

Ephesians. The meaning of this power language, however, is radically re-defined by the example of Christ, a point that is missed if headship is defined as source.

The word "submission" (*hypotasso*) is a military term that means to order or arrange properly. It is concerned with the right "lining up" or alignment of troops for battle. Troops that are properly "lined up" or "ordered" are said to be "in submission." They are ready to function as a unit in battle. Similarly, a wife who submits is lined up, ready to function as a unit with her husband.

THE LITERARY CONTEXT OF EPHESIANS 5:21-33

Ephesians 4:17—6:9 exhorts Christians to live in contrast to the lifestyle of the world. Paul warns against a relapse into pagan conduct. The church is to show a striking unlikeness to immoral paganism. To help the church achieve this goal, Paul outlines the ethical standards that are to characterize the church. The first section, 4:17—5:20, describes the difference between Christianity and paganism: truth/falsehood, light/darkness, saintliness/immorality, wisdom/folly, spirit/devil, etc. The point is that there are two distinct peoples living in the world, each with its own ethic. The church is to walk in the truth, light, wisdom and spirit of Christ. Ephesians 5:21—6:9 discusses the meaning of the Christian walk for household relationships. The husband/wife relationship is the first addressed in 5:21-33. The question is whether Messiah Jesus and the community of the church in any way influence the lives of men and women in their most intimate and critical relationship.

STRUCTURE OF EPHESIANS 5:21-31

The text begins and ends with a concern for reverence and respect. Verse 21 asks wives to show reverence for Christ; verse 33 to show reverence for their husbands. This is a literary technique which says that the passage is concerned with issues of reverence and respect. The second mention of respect for the husband is clearly dependent on the first, respect for Christ. So the point of 5:21-33 is reverence and respect in the household.

Secondly, the text begins and ends with exhortations supported by a single motivation—Christ. Reverence for Christ is the motivation for mutual submission (v. 21). Christ's headship of the church is the standard of the wife's submission to her husband (vv. 22-24). The Messiah's love is the ground and measure of the husband's love for his wife (v. 25a). The unity of Christ with his body is the basis for the husband's love of his wife as himself (vv. 28-30). Paul says nothing about the relationship of the two partners in marriage unless he can show a messianic and churchly basis. Paul's intention is to show that Christ and the church give husband and wife the basis and example to live in that peace to which God has called them. The peace between human and human, and between God and human, which Paul described in Chapter 2, shall be extended to the conduct of husband and wife.

Thirdly, it is important to note that Paul directs commands only to husbands, not to wives. The only true commands appear in verses 25 and 33; husbands are commanded to love their wives. Wives are not commanded to submit to their husbands; they are invited to do so.

Verse 21 — Mutual Submission

The passage is introduced by an exhortation to mutual subordination. Literally the sentence begins, "being continuously subordinate." Paul's concern is that wives and husbands be properly ordered, that they be mutually "ordering under." The translation of "being continuously subordinate" as a command to "be submissive" is alien to the sense and intent of the verb. It appeals to free and responsible people to heed voluntarily, not by the breaking of the will.

The object of the verbal phrase "being subordinate" is the phrase "to one another." The "ordering under" is to be in relationship to one another. "Being subordinate" does not refer to the ordering of an inferior to a superior, which is the normal use of the word, but an ordering of relationships between equals.

The context for this mutual ordering is "in the reverence of Christ," literally, "in the fear of Christ." This is the only use of the phrase "in the fear of Christ" in the New Testament. It carries the Old Testament sense of the "fear of God." God is feared when revealed in mighty deeds of salvation for Israel. Their appropriate reaction is awe before majesty, rejoicing over victory, and fear before mighty power. In Deuteronomy "the fear of the Lord" and "love" are used as synonyms. Both the fear of God and the love of God mean to live faithfully according to God's covenant and law. Husbands and wives are exhorted to subordinate themselves voluntarily to each other out of a profound sense of faithfulness to Christ.

The point of the text is silenced whenever the dominating position of the request to "be continuously subordinate to one another" over the entire unit is neglected. The issue is not ordering by rank but the

mutual ordering of equals in intimate relationship with
Christ and each other in a marriage relationship.

Verses 22-24 — The Mutual Subordination of the Wife

Verse 22 does not have a verb; it reads literally "the
wives to their own husbands as to the Lord." The phrase
is dependent on the "being subordinate" verb of verse
21. The first example of mutual subordination is the
wife. The wife is asked to subordinate herself voluntarily to her husband within the framework of mutual subordination. She is treated as a person responsible for
her own ethical decisions and is called to take a stance.
This is a very revolutionary development in ancient ethics. Wives generally were not recognized as ethical de-
cision-makers independent of their husbands, but as
subordinates to be commanded to action by their husbands without the involvement of their will.

The object of the women's subordination is not men
in general, but "their own husbands." Verse 22 does not
say that women are inferior to men. Paul is discussing
only the special relationship between husband and wife.
Paul is announcing a drastic restriction of women's subordination; it is due only to "their own husbands" just as
the husband's marital love is due only to his wife (vv.
25, 28, 33). Furthermore, Paul does not use the word
"obey" or "serve" to describe the wife's relationship to
her husband, but "ordering under." She is a person who
stands on the same level with her husband and is able
to make her own decisions.

The motivation for the wife's mutual subordination
is "as to the Lord." A wife's commitment to order herself
under her husband should be of the same quality as her
commitment to Christ. The parallel text in Colossians

3:18 makes this even more explicit: "Wives, be subject to your husbands, as is fitting in the Lord." Paul does not refer to nature, to general standards of decency, to the law, or to the Fall for the ground of his exhortation. Only Jesus is the source, standard, and motivation for a wife's "ordering under." That also means that Jesus is the limit and reward of a positive decision to be mutually subordinate.

Verse 23 provides the rationale for the wife's submission. It is rooted in redemption, in Christ as the head of the church. The husband is the head of the wife, meaning the head as leader or authority. But the husband is not the absolute authority over the wife. He is the head "as Christ." Christ is the original model of headship. Christ is the model, the measure, and the limit of the husband's headship over the wife. Thus, a very qualified headship is attributed to the husband. Christ is made the head of the church "for the church" (1:22) and as the Savior of the church (v. 23). He proves himself the head by saving. The Christ/church relation is the model of the husband's headship.

Verse 24 reverses the role-model example. The church/Christ relation is the model of the wife's subordination. Just as the church chooses to "order itself under" Christ, so the wife chooses to be subordinate to her husband.

The nature of mutual subordination for the wife is startling. Wives are not commanded to obey their husbands or to submit to the authority of their husbands. Wives are not ordered to "be subordinate" to men or to their own husbands. Wives are invited to choose subordination. Furthermore, the call to subordination is qualified at least three times: (1) the opening call for mutual subordination; (2) the limitation of subordination to "her own" husband; (3) the definition of the wife's subordination in terms of the church's subordination to Christ.

Verses 25-33 — The Mutual Subordination of the Husband

Verse 25 defines the meaning of mutual subordination for husbands with an imperative. The only commands in the passage are to husbands, not to wives. The husband is commanded to love the wife. Mutual subordination for him is defined as loving the wife. Love is defined by Christ's giving up of self for the good of the church. Jesus alone is the origin and the criterion of marital love as mutual subordination. Love is not defined by a principle, but by the person of the Messiah. Husbands are exhorted to give themselves up for their wives. When Christ is upheld as the model for husbands, it is not his power, lordship, or authority which is presented, but his humility and servanthood. Headship language is turned on its head. Power is redefined as love and self-giving, not as exercising authority over another person.

The head/body metaphor is changed to the groom/bride relationship in verse 27. The bridegroom's love has the will and power to effect a total transformation. He confers a dignity and wholeness on the bride which she does not possess on her own.

Verse 28 translates literally as "in the same manner also husbands owe it to love their wives for they are their bodies." The "also" before "husbands" makes it clear that the "so" or "in the same manner" at the beginning of verse 28 refers to the love of Christ described in verses 25-27, not to love of self. The husband's love is compared with Christ's love (as in v. 25), not with a man's natural love of his own body. Only after the husband's love has been compared with Christ's love does Paul describe the effect of such love on the wife. She is her loving husband's body. Mutual subordination for the husband means loving the wife so that the two become so intimately one that he can call her "his body," and call his love for her, love for his body.

Furthermore, the logic of the husband's love for his wife is very important. The movement is not from love of self to love of one's wife to love of Christ. Rather, it is from the love shown by Christ, to the love shown for the wife to the love of the husband for himself. This manner of reasoning about marriage was radical in Paul's day, as it is in the twentieth century.

Verses 29-30 explain verse 28 further, "for no one ever has hated his own flesh." No husband hates his wife, for she is his body. Rather, he continuously nurtures and cares (notice the shift from past to continuous present tense) for her. For the third time in this passage (vv. 23 and 25) the phrase "just as the Messiah" is found in the second half of a statement. It attributes to Christ the basis for and model of the behavior expected of husbands. When Christ's care for the church is the model for husbands, they will care for their wives and hatred will have no place. What the church experiences from Christ is what wives should expect from their husbands. Nothing is asked of husbands that has not first been realized in the church.

Verse 31 quotes Genesis 2:24, now applied to the Christ/church model of verses 29b-30. The phrase "for this reason," which in Genesis 2 referred to the creation of Eve out of Adam, now refers to the Christ/church relationship described in verses 25-30. Christ's salvation of the church fulfills all that was said of Adam and Eve in Genesis 2. The miracle of union of husband and wife predicted in Genesis 2 has occurred in the Christ/church relationship. The concept is so revolutionary that Paul calls it a "mystery," an end-time secret previously hidden but now revealed. Earlier in Ephesians Paul writes that the mystery concerns the incorporation of Gentiles into God's people. Christ's relation to the church, which includes the incorporation of diverse peoples, is the original model of the marriage relationship. Mutual submission pertains to the very nature of Christ and his relationship to the church in all its diversity.

What is implied by the application of the Christ/church relationship to marriage in verses 28-32 is made explicit in verse 33, "in sum, one by one, each one of you must love his wife as himself." The strong command, "must love," the emphatic inclusion of "every one," and the address to husbands before the wives distinguish verse 33 from verses 22-25, where the wives were exhorted first. The sharpness of Paul's address to the husbands in comparison with the soft manner of encouraging the wives indicates that Paul considers the men more reluctant to show love for their wives than for the wives to subordinate themselves to their husbands. "And the wife in order that she may reverence the husband" is a hesitant statement compared with the direct words to the husband. Paul seems to say that "I expect that the wife will be enabled to reverence her husband by his behavior toward her, but I do not command it."

REFLECTIONS

Ephesians 5:21-33 concerns family order, not church order. This text cannot be used to argue for the submission of women in the church. The text says nothing about church order.

Paul's concern for family order is directed more to husbands than to wives. The demands on husbands are significantly heavier than on wives. Wives are asked to order themselves appropriately as ethical agents in a relationship of equals. Only forty words in three verses are addressed to wives. Furthermore, wives are not ordered to submit to "the order of marriage." Paul has no theology of orders. The only order for Paul is the Christ-centered one. The Christ/church relation is Paul's substitute for the law of marriage. The call for submission is a limited one, to the husband only. Women are not inferior persons who must submit to all men.

Husbands are commanded to love. Ninety-two words in eight verses are addressed to them. Paul commands husbands to love three times: verses 25a, 28, 33. Love and love alone is the husband's critical obligation to his wife. Further, Paul does not leave it to the husband's imagination to define love. The example of Christ defines the nature of love. Headship and power language is redefined in the most radical terms. To be the head is to love and to give up self for the sake of the other, the wife.

Ephesians 5:21-33 is a profound and radical family order text. Headship language here and in 1 Corinthians 11 cannot be used to argue that women are inferior or that women must submit to male leadership. Headship language concerns the husband/wife relationship, not the woman/man relationship in church leadership.

Furthermore, in the upside down world of Christ's kingdom, headship means taking the lead in self-sacrifice. The hostility of the fall has been overcome. There is a new creation order and community, the model of Christ and the body of the church. All things are made new in the new creation.

The problem in Ephesians 5:21-33 is not women, but men. The modern church would do well to let Paul's vision for men and husbands correct our distortions. To take Ephesians 5 seriously would certainly address the family crisis of our time, and the problem of abuse of women in the home and in the church. The church would do well to use Ephesians 5 as Paul intended it, to call men to change.

SUGGESTIONS FOR READING

Barth, Markus. Ephesians 4—6. Doubleday, 1974.

Bilezikian, Gilbert. Beyond Sex Roles. Baker, 1985.

Clark, S.B. Man and Woman in Christ. Servant Books, 1980.

Evans, Mary J. Woman in the Bible. InterVarsity Press, 1983.

Hurley, J.B. Man and Woman in Biblical Perspective. Zondervan, 1981.

Michelsen, Alvera, ed. Women, Authority and the Bible. InterVarsity, 1986.

Park, David M. "The Structure and Authority in Marriage: An Examination of Hupotasso and Kephale in Ephesians 5:21-33." Evangelical Quarterly 59 (1987): 117-124.

I PERMIT NO WOMAN TO TEACH

John E. Toews

Women in Church Leadership:
1 Timothy 2:8-15

Corrie ten Boom of Holland spent time in a Nazi concentration camp because of her family's involvement with hiding Jews during the war. After her release from the death camp, she set out for the United States "to carry the Gospel as a missionary to the Americans," she writes. The opportunities for speaking, however, did not come easily. "The Americans were polite and some of them were interested, but none wanted me to come and speak ... No one was interested in a middle-aged spinster woman from Holland who wanted to preach." After the endorsement of an influential Christian man, she told her story time and again, always with an evangelistic thrust. Corrie's ministry entailed three decades of speaking in more than sixty countries, beginning in the United States. She and other women like Joni Eareckson represent a new breed of

female speakers whose subject matter comes primarily
out of their own struggles in the Christian life. — Ruth
A. Tucker and Walter Liefeld, Daughters of the Church

The critical biblical text for the question of women in
ministry is 1 Timothy 2:11-15. However, its interpretation is filled with problems. The traditional reading assumes that the thrust of the passage is proper order in the church, and its point the subordination of
women. An alternative interpretation argues that wom-
en are forbidden to teach only if they are unlearned or if
they link teaching with sexual seduction. A third interpretation refers the passage to family relationships and
not to issues of church order. [1]

THE TRADITIONAL INTERPRETATION: THE SUBORDINATION OF WOMEN

The traditional interpretation of verses 11-12 teaches that women are to be silent in the church, to be subordinate to men, not to teach in the church, and not to
exercise authority over men. Two reasons are given for
this interpretation. First, teaching involves the exercise
of authority; it is a governing function restricted to men.
Secondly, women are not to exercise authority over men.
This reading of verse 12b assumes that the word *authentein*, the only occurrence of this word in the New
Testament, means "to exercise authority." Its precise
meaning is ambiguous. It may forbid women to exercise
authority over men, or to usurp authority from men, or
to improperly use authority over men. Despite this acknowledged ambiguity, traditional interpreters understand the word to forbid all exercise of authority.

---

1 For a longer version of this article with documentation, see "Women in
Church Leadership. 1 Timothy 2:11-15: A Reconsideration," The Bible
and the Church: Essays in Honor of Dr. David Ewert (Kindred Press,
1988), pp. 75-93.

The issue in verses 11-12 then, according to this interpretation, is the proper relationship of men and women in the church. Women are to be silent and not to teach in the church because such activity constitutes "exercising authority" over men.

Verses 13-14 provide the reasons women are to be silent.

Verse 13 is believed to assert that because Adam was created first, males are superior throughout history.

Verse 14 states the cause as the fall. Eve's deception, in this reading, changed the nature of womanhood and made all women more susceptible to deception than men. Therefore, it is inappropriate for women to teach and exercise authority.

Verse 15 is a very difficult verse, and its meaning remains uncertain. Most evangelicals struggle between reading the words "woman will be saved through childbearing" as a reference to the birth of the Messiah, or as a statement about the proper sphere of women's activities and the good works of verse 10. Both views are problematic. The text does not speak of the Messiah, and the second view involves a theology of salvation by works that runs contrary to Paul's teaching.

Problems with the Traditional Interpretation

The traditional reading has been challenged for a variety of reasons.

(1) It fails to recognize that the critical words in the text have more than one meaning, as the standard Greek dictionary indicates. The traditional interpretation reads each word in the most restrictive way possible, even when this is a secondary meaning or is consistently used differently by Paul in other passages.

(2) The traditional interpretation contradicts at least six other teachings of Paul which then must be resolved.

a. A radical differentiation between men's and women's roles contradicts the principle of the mutuality of the sexes in 1 Corinthians 7 and Ephesians 5.

b. The prohibition of women teaching contradicts Colossians 3:16 and 1 Corinthians 14:26, which state that the teaching ministry is open to all qualified believers. The word "teach" in Colossians is the same as in 1 Timothy 2. The teaching ministry is open to all on the same basis as the other ministries listed in Colossians 3: authority to forgive (v. 13), to love (v. 14), to admonish and to make music (v. 16). None are restricted on the basis of sex. Verses 18-19 differentiate instructions on the basis of gender. Thus Paul differentiates between men and women when necessary. If a ban on women teachers was important for all the churches, it would have been in order for Paul to remind the churches of this restriction in the context of a general invitation to share in Christian ministries, including teaching.

c. The prohibition of teaching contradicts the freedom for women to exercise the more authoritative ministry of prophecy. The most authoritative ministries in the New Testament are apostle, prophet, and teacher. In every catalog of the gifts (Rom. 12, 1 Cor. 12, Eph. 4) teaching is always listed after prophecy. Women are free to prophesy (1 Cor. 11:5; Acts 2:16-18; 21:9). Prophecy is teaching by inspiration rather than from tradition. It is a more authoritative ministry than teaching. Apostles and prophets constitute the foundation of the church, whereas teaching is not so defined. Paul's teaching is inconsistent if 1 Timothy 2 forbids women to teach though they are free to exercise the more authoritative ministries in the church.

d. The reading of the Adam/Eve illustration contradicts Paul's other uses of Adam and Eve. Adam's creation before Eve is used only one other time in the New Testament, 1 Corinthians 11:8-10. Adam's creation before Eve is declared meaningless because "in the Lord" both are interdependent. Therefore, the woman can worship God independently of the man (as long as she is appropriately dressed). Here Eve is held accountable for the fall of the human race. But in Romans 5 and 1 Corinthians 15 Adam is held responsible. Paul, therefore, sounds discordant in the traditional interpretation of 1 Timothy.

e. If the ban on women teaching is a retribution for the fall, then Adam's responsibility for the fall should involve a restriction for men. To prohibit women but not men from teaching as a judgment for the fall really means that women are excluded from full salvation because of Eve's sin. Furthermore, if the ban on women teaching is a function of the fall, there is no explanation why this ministry is chosen rather than the more authoritative ministry of prophecy.

f. Finally, this interpretation contradicts Paul's own practice of including women in his ministries. Paul names sixteen women as "co-workers" in his ministries (Rom. 16; Phil. 4:2-3; Col. 4:15; Phlm. 2; Acts 16:14-15). The terms used to describe the activities of these women are normally associated with leadership roles: "minister" (Rom. 16:1); "ruler" (Rom. 16:2); "my fellow worker in Christ Jesus" (Rom. 16:3; Phil. 4:3); "apostle" (Rom. 16:7); "worked hard in the Lord" (Rom. 16:6, 12); "contended at my side for the cause of the gospel" (Phil. 4:3); "explaining the way of the Lord more accurately" (Acts 18:26). (See Chapters 2 and 7.)

These contradictions create problems for a coherent reading of Paul. Any overall interpretation of the ministry of women in the church, and of the 1 Timothy 2 text, must create a more consistent interpretation of Paul.

(3) That this prohibition is mentioned only once in Scripture is problematic. The exclusion of women from a significant ministry is a major stance that should be repeated in other writings dealing with the exercise of ministries in the church. The texts dealing with such ministries (Rom. 12, 1 Cor. 12, Eph. 4) do not hint at the exclusion of women. In fact, it is clear that women are gifted and empowered for diverse ministries of the church. The gifts and ministries of the Spirit are never differentiated on the basis of gender.

(4) The problem of verse 15 ("she shall be saved through childbirth") calls the entire traditional interpretation into question. If a key statement in any text cannot be integrated into the overall meaning of the text, as well as into the other teachings of the Scripture, that suggests the text has not been properly interpreted.

AN ALTERNATIVE INTERPRETATION: NO UNLEARNED WOMAN SHALL TEACH

A series of evangelical scholars are attempting an alternative interpretation to resolve some of the problems of the traditional interpretation.

The Historical Context of 1 Timothy 2:11-15

The Pastoral Letters address problems of false teaching in young missionary churches (1 Tim. 1:3-11, 19-20; 4:1-10; 6:3-4, 20f.; 2 Tim. 1:15; 2:14, 16-18, 23; 3:1-9, 13; 4:3-4; Titus 1:10-16; 3:9-11). 1 Timothy was written to stop false teaching (1:3). It is clear that women were involved in the false teachings (1 Tim. 3:11, 5:11-15; 2 Tim. 3:6-7), and that some women were going

from house to house spreading these teachings (1 Tim.
5:13). Young widows especially were among those influenced by the false teachers.

It is important to note that Ephesus was one of the
centers of female religion in the ancient world. It was
known as "the bastion of the female spiritual principle."
One temple was dedicated to Artemis (or Diana) and a
second to Aphrodite (Venus). The goddess Artemis represented the most powerful expression of the Great
Mother. She took second place to no other god. In the religious culture of Ephesus, woman was created before
man. The role of the male in procreation was un-
important. Descent was claimed through the mother.
The genealogy of the mother, not the father, provided a
person with rank. Women were thought to possess special affinity for the divine and served as mediators between the human and the divine. Sacred prostitution,
therefore, was a special feature of religion in Ephesus
and of the divine/human mediation. Temple prostitution
effected a union with the goddess, thus bringing salvation and fertility. Ephesus boasted thousands of
prostitutes.

By the end of the first century, a gnostic world view
was taught in Ephesus. This view stated that female activity was responsible for the creation of the universe,
and that Eve pre-existed Adam, who was created from
her side. She could procreate without Adam and she was
his instructor. In addition, laws in Ephesus forbade
women, with the exception of prostitutes, to wear the
adornment forbidden to Christian women in 1 Timothy
2:9.

Finally, a general link between teaching and sexual
activity existed in the ancient world. Male teachers engaged in homosexuality with male students. Female

teachers concluded their teaching by announcing their availability for sex with their students.

We must remember that 1 Timothy was written to a church in a culture dominated by false teaching and a focus on female sexuality. Paul was attempting to correct situations that involved women serving as false teachers, acting immorally, dressing as prostitutes, and arguing about questions of origins (genealogies).

The Literary Context of 1 Timothy 2:11-15

Chapter 2 begins with "therefore" followed by instructions that are a consequence of the concern for combating false teaching in Chapter 1. The thesis of Chapter 2 is that the gospel is for all people (vv. 1, 4-6, 7). Therefore, the first order of business is offering prayers for all people, including the authorities.

In verse 8 the concern shifts to particular controversies in Ephesus affecting the credibility of the gospel. The main issue is improper conduct: men are gathering for prayer but fighting instead. Women are dressing inappropriately, teaching before they are knowledgeable, and linking their teaching to sexual activity.

The issue of teaching is preceded by an exhortation regarding proper dress. The critical concern of the adornment texts is fidelity in marriage. Women's adornment and submission to husbands are linked in common instructions in the ancient world. They are two sides of the same coin. The adornment texts uniformly speak in favor of modest clothes and of a wife's submission to her husband. Expensive adornment was a sign of sexual infidelity, and in Ephesus the adornment question was also linked to prostitution.

The Meaning of the Words in 1 Timothy 2:11-15

The standard New Testament Greek dictionary indicates that interpreters must make important choices of meaning for the key words in this text. Optional meanings are indicated in the order of preference given in the dictionary.

The word translated "silence" in verses 11 and 12 means (1) quietness, as in peace or harmony, or (2) quiet, as in silence. The word "subjection," also in verse 11, is a military term that means "in order." It is concerned with the right "lining up" of troops for battle. Properly ordered troops are said to be "in subjection."

"I am not allowing" (v. 12) is the primary meaning of *epitrepo*. But the secondary meaning, "order" or "instruct," is preferred when the word is used with the infinitive form of the verb. "To teach" and "to sexually seduce" ("to exercise authority" in the traditional interpretation) are infinitives. So in verse 12 the word has something to do with proper ordering or lining up.

The critical word in verse 12 is *authentein*, traditionally translated as "to exercise authority." It is a compound word from "self" and "thrust." The basic meaning is "to thrust oneself." The word went through three stages of meaning in the ancient world. The earliest meaning is to "commit murder or suicide," that is, to thrust a weapon into someone. The second stage of meaning, from 300 B.C. to A.D. 300 (the period of our text) is to "thrust oneself sexually" or to "desire sexually." This meaning is used in an intertestamental writing known as the Wisdom of Solomon 12:6. John Chrysostom, one of the earliest church fathers to comment on 1 Timothy 2:12, translates the text as "I forbid a woman to teach and to engage in fertility practices with a man." Another early church father, Clement of

Alexandria (A.D. 200), uses the word with the same meaning. The third stage of meaning, which begins around A.D. 300, is to "thrust oneself to rule" or to "usurp authority." Traditional interpreters have taken a later meaning and read it back into the New Testament, but the word must be defined by the usage of its period, and thus refers to sexual intercourse in the text.

The "for" at the beginning of verse 13 is normally an explanatory term, not a causal word as in the traditional interpretation. It introduces an explanation or illustration, not a statement of cause; it means "for example" not "because." The other "double meaning" word in verse 13 is the word "created." It can mean (1) to create something or (2) to form with understanding. Thus, it can refer to Adam's creation by God or to his education by God.

The word "saved" in verse 15 normally means "preserved for good" or "preserved from disaster and affliction." In the New Testament, and especially in Paul, it most often refers to "salvation from sin and death," but it can still be used in its secular sense.

The Meaning of 2:11-15

Verse 11 - "Let a woman be discipled peacefully in all orderliness."

The lead sentence states that women are to be discipled and taught. This instruction represents a radical teaching in the ancient world. With a few exceptions, women were not taught. But in the church, women are to be taught.

Women's learning is to be characterized by two things. They are to learn peacefully or harmoniously. The connotation of silence is not present. Secondly, the learning is to be orderly. Submission is not the issue, but orderliness in learning. Women are to be learners during their instructional times; they are not to assert themselves prematurely as teachers.

This teaching addresses the style of female worship in the ancient world. The worship of women was different from that of men. They often worshiped different gods in different temples on different days and in different ways. Women were noisy and uninhibited in worship while the men were sedate and silent. The worship of women was often indecent and indiscreet. When these women became Christians, they had to learn a different mode of worship.

Verse 12 - "And I am not lining up (or I am not permitting) a woman to teach or to sexually seduce a man, but to be in peacefulness."

Though Paul is instructing women in Ephesus not to teach, the verb "lining up" here does not refer to a continuing state. Paul, more than any other New Testament writer, separated his personal advice for a particular situation from permanently valid instruction. He identifies a command of the Lord as such (e.g., 1 Cor. 7:6, 10, 12, 25, 40), or he explicitly states a command to be observed in all the churches (e.g., 1 Cor. 11:16; 14:33, 34, 36). In contrast, when Paul gave personal advice, he used the first person singular verb form (e.g., 1 Cor 7:6, 7, 8, 12, 17, 25, 26, 28, 29, 32, 35, 40). In verse 12 Paul uses the typical verbal form for giving personal counsel. It is his advice for the particular situation in Ephesus, and cannot be generalized into a command for all time. Paul could have written "I will never permit" if that is what he intended. Furthermore, when Paul does specify a timeless instruction, he usually indicates this with phrases such as "in behalf of all" (1 Tim. 2:1) or "in every place" (1 Tim. 2:8). He gives no indication that the instruction for women not to teach is to be understood as a continuing prohibition. Rather, he is offering instruction for the particular situation in Ephesus.

The word "teach" can refer to authoritative Christian teaching, to teaching one another, to human teaching, or to Jewish teaching. The teaching described here is teaching one another. Paul does not want unlearned women to be teaching men. More specifically, Paul does not want women to be teaching men and sexually seducing them, which was the practice in the church in Thyatira (Rev. 2:20). Instead, the women are to be peaceful or harmonious. They are to be in the community as gracious learners, not seductive teachers.

Clearly the instruction of verses 11-12 is that women be peaceful learners because it is the first thing said in verse 11 and the last thing said in verse 12. A literal translation indicates the poetic structure of the text and underlines this emphasis:

> A woman in *peacefulness* let learn
> in all orderliness
> to teach not I am lining up
> nor to sexually seduce a man
> but to be in *peacefulness*.

Verses 13-14 - "For example, Adam was formed with understanding first, and then Eve. And Adam was not deceived, but the woman was deceived having become a transgressor."

The example of Adam and Eve offers a Jewish commentary on the creation story. The example makes one point, not two, as in most commentaries. The issue is education as a safeguard against deception. Creation and then the fall are not two different events and causes. Adam was taught first; his understanding was formed first, and then Eve's. In other words, verses 13-14 present a statement about the order of Adam's and Eve's education, not the order of their creation. Adam was not deceived because he knew better. Eve was misled because she was not properly taught. Adam's being created first makes him more knowledgeable and thus more responsible, not more righteous.

The point of the illustration is that women must be taught or they will again be led astray, as in fact was happening (5:15). This interpretation fits the one other reference to Eve's being deceived, 2 Corinthians 11:3. There Eve is an illustration of the dangers of being led astray by unauthorized teachers.

Verse 15 - "And she will be saved by means of the childbearing if they remain in faith and love and holiness with reasonable judgment."

"Saved" is used here in its non-theological meaning, to preserve from natural dangers and afflictions, to keep in good condition.

But from what will the woman be preserved in childbearing? Interpreters have offered two proposals. First, she will be preserved from the theological barrier that outlaws her from teaching. In childbearing woman demonstrates her divinely ordered preeminence over man, even as man's prior creation and education shows his preeminence over woman. Paul's argument here is interpreted as similar to 1 Corinthians 11:8-9. Woman is saved from her subordinate status by bearing children. Woman assumes a prior position to the man as his source. While woman is created and educated second, she is first in the birthing sequence. Childbearing then serves the healing function of counterbalancing man's prior creation and education.

Although such reasoning seems strange to us, it shows that Paul was struggling to express a fundamental equality between the sexes in categories that were understandable at that time. Each sex is logically prior in equally significant, but different, ways.

The second proposal interprets salvation to mean protection in the intensified pain of the birthing process. That is, salvation addresses the pain of the curse in Genesis 3.

Whatever the precise object of the salvation, the verse concludes by promising woman's full restoration if women and men—"they" (plural, not singular as at the beginning of the verse)—live faithfully.

Verses 11-15, therefore, teach that women are to be educated before they teach. Women are forbidden to teach if they are unlearned or if they link teaching with sexual seduction.

An Assessment of the Debate

The nontraditional interpretation provides an historical context for the concern of the text. It takes seriously the ambiguous language used, and it resolves the problem of contradictions with other Pauline teachings. The interpretation of verse 15 offers more hope of contextual meaning. On strictly interpretive and exegetical grounds, this reading is preferable to the traditional one.

But the debate illustrates a critical problem in interpretation. Evangelical scholars are unable to agree on what Paul is saying. This lack of interpretive consensus is an evangelical family affair; it is not an evangelical/liberal dispute. Most critical scholars resolve the problems in the alternative interpretations by declaring 1 Timothy non-Pauline and nonauthoritative for the church. The evangelical community is deeply divided over the real meaning of 1 Timothy 2:11-15. Are women only prohibited from teaching men, or are they prohibited from teaching anyone? Does the prohibition apply to women everywhere in all times, or only to women addressed in the culturally specific situation of first-century Ephesus? The wide and intensive disagreements among evangelical scholars indicates that both readings are problematic. When two alternative readings of the text are so diametrically opposite, they usually share a common assumption which if challenged creates the possibility of a different reading.

ANOTHER POSSIBLE READING: A CONCERN FOR FAMILY RELATIONSHIPS

The traditional and the nonrestrictive interpretations are built on one common assumption: both assume that verses 11-15 concern public worship. This assumption is based on two more assumptions. First, verses 1-7 refer to prayer in public worship, and secondly, the exhortation for men to pray with hands lifted refers to public prayer. "In every place" in verse 8 is assumed to mean "every place where the church gathers for worship." The rest of the chapter is read as a discussion of public worship on the basis of these assumptions.

A Challenge to the Common Assumption
The assumption ought to be challenged on at least six grounds.

(1) In the Old Testament and Judaism, the father, as head of the family, led prayers for the household and taught the members of the extended family. Everything

exhorted in Chapter 2:1ff. is instruction given to fathers.

(2) "In every place" is used three other times by Paul (1 Thes. 1:8; 1 Cor. 1:2; 2 Cor. 2:4), and never means "whenever the church gathers for worship," nor is it a synonym for "in every church." The phrase refers to the world, to every place where the action described is occurring. In 1 Timothy 2:8 Paul is talking about men praying wherever they are. Nothing suggests a public worship context.

(3) Who is to submit in verse 11 has never been clear. The Adam and Eve illustration suggests the wife is to submit to the husband. But scholars have assumed it is men in general. Nothing in the context, however, suggests the reference is anything other than the husband of the Adam and Eve illustration.

(4) The singular "she" in verses 11-15a has always puzzled scholars. It should be plural for women in public worship.

(5) The linkage between adornment/sexual fidelity and marital submission in the adornment texts has been ignored by nearly all interpreters.

(6) The shift from the singular "she" to the plural "they" in verse 15 has troubled scholars. The assumption is that the shift is from woman as singular to women as plural. Thus, if women as a collective body will live by faith, love and holiness, they will be saved.

A New Reading

I suggest that 1 Timothy 2:8-15 refers to family relationships.

Verse 8 - The lifting of hands in prayer is a common practice in Judaism whether in public or private prayer. Husbands are exhorted to pray with proper posture and disposition.

Verses 9-10 - The issue of the adornment of women is concerned with husband/wife relationships. Wives are to live monogamously with their husbands.

Verse 11 - The words translated "woman" in verses 11 and 12 and "man" in verse 12 are the common words for wife and husband. The only exhortation in the New Testament for women to "be submissive," and "to order themselves appropriately," is to married women (Eph. 5:24; Col. 3:18; 1 Pet. 3:1). Husbands are to teach their wives. Wives are to learn peacefully and without the use of sexual manipulation.

It is hard to imagine how radical this teaching was in the ancient world. The home was the private domain, literally, the "domain of the idiot." The public assembly, called the *ecclesia* (our word for church), was a place of higher education. The home was the center of a woman's power, the public place was the center of a man's power. The two did not intersect. Besides Paul, only a few men like Musonius Rufus, a Roman philosopher of Paul's time, issue a radical challenge that women be treated as fully equal with men and that they be educated. Both assert that the public sphere should be moved into the private.

Paul wants to give content to the marital relationship. That also is a radical stance. It was common for men to be 30 or more years of age at the time of marriage and for women to be in their teens. Paul's exhortation for husbands to teach their young wives is revolutionary.

Verse 12-13 - The relationship between husband and wife is illustrated in the example of Adam and Eve. When Eve, who was uninformed because of her subsequent creation, taught Adam, she led herself and Adam astray.

Verse 15 - The reference to salvation through child-bearing is a promise either that the wife will be saved from her subordinate status by childbearing or that she will be preserved from disaster in childbearing. The plural pronoun of verse 15b refers to the husband and wife, picking up the idea of Adam and Eve from the previous statement. The wife will be preserved in childbirth if the husband and wife together live by faith, love and holiness. Christian discipleship is the equal responsibility of the husband and wife together.

Proposed Translation of 2:8-15

Verse 8 - I wish, therefore, the husbands to pray in every place lifting holy hands without anger or disputation.

Verse 9 - Likewise, also wives dress with good taste and modesty and dress with good judgment, not with plaited hair and gold or pearls or expensive clothes,

Verse 10 - but as fitting wives who promise godliness through good works.

Verse 11 - Let a wife be discipled peacefully in all orderliness.

Verse 12 - And I am not permitting a wife to teach or sexually manipulate her husband, but to be in peacefulness.

Verses 13-14 - For example, Adam was formed with understanding first and then Eve. And Adam was not deceived but the woman was deceived having become a transgressor.

Verse 15 - And she (the wife) shall be saved through childbearing if they (husband and wife) remain in faith and love and holiness with good judgment.

Summary

The focus of the text is on the husband/wife relationship, not public worship. Therefore, this text ought not to be used to address the question of women's roles in public ministry. The point of the text is that the unlearned wife is to be taught by her husband, thus giving theological content to the marriage relationship. She is not to teach her husband or to link teaching him with sexual manipulation. Furthermore, the wife should not participate in prostitution, sacred or otherwise, but live faithfully with her husband as together they seek to be true disciples of Jesus.

SUGGESTIONS FOR READING

Bilezikian, Gilbert. Beyond Sex Roles. Baker, 1985.

Clark, S.B. Man and Woman in Christ. Servant Books, 1980.

Evans, Mary J. Woman in the Bible. InterVarsity, 1983.

Fee, Gordon. "Issues in Evangelical Hermeneutics, Part III: The Great Watershed — Intentionality and Particularity/ Eternality: 1 Timothy 2:8-15 as a Test Case." Crux 26 (1990): 31-37.

Gritz, Sharon Hodgin. Paul, Women Teachers and the Mother Goddess at Ephesus. A Study of 1 Timothy 2:9-15 in Light of the Religious and Cultural Milieu of the First Century. University Press of America, 1991.

Hurley, J.B. Man and Woman in Biblical Perspective. Zondervan, 1981.

Michelsen, Alvera, ed. Women, Authority and the Bible. InterVarsity, 1986.

Toews, John E. "Women in Church Leadership: 1 Timothy
    2:11-15, A Reconsideration." The Bible and the Church.
    A.J. Dueck, H.J. Giesbrecht, V.G. Shillington, eds.
    Kindred Press, 1988: 75-93.

Marilyn G. Peters

The Relation of Renewal and Institutionalization

Anneken Jans, a Dutch Anabaptist, suffered death by drowning in 1539. An heiress of a considerable fortune, she sacrificed everything for her faith, and at the age of 24, was baptized with her husband. Because she was singing a hymn, she was arrested and charged with sectarianism. At the place of execution she pled with someone in the crowd to adopt her 15-month-old son Esaias. She offered a full purse for the child's support. A baker with six children of his own volunteered. She left her young son a letter inspiring him to faithful performance as a Christian. —
Mennonite Encyclopedia

The history of women in ministry in the church is a story of paradox. New and reform movements tend to open and encourage the ministry of women. As the movements institutionalize, however, women are often restricted in ministry, and denied the ministries they performed earlier.

THE EARLY CHURCH

No uniform policy or practice regarding women in ministry prevailed in the first centuries. The historical evidence—writings, mosaics and frescoes—indicate that the ministry of women flourished in the early church. Women were deacons and ministers in the church. The same evidence reports the emergence of negative attitudes toward women—the cause of sin and seducers—and restriction or even prohibition of the ministry of women.

Regardless of attitudes, women died for the faith just as men did. Eusebius narrates the martyrdom of Blandina in 177 A.D. as proof that God uses and honors the ministry of women. Her torture was long and intense, and concluded with her being hanged in the shape of a cross in an amphitheater. Other Christians, who also were being persecuted in the same amphitheater, looked to her as the image of Christ for sustenance in their own suffering.

MEDIEVAL CHRISTIANITY

Two conflicting images of women emerged in the Middle Ages. The most prominent image was of women as evil and inferior. They were viewed as defective males, and thus subordinate and inferior to men. Women were assumed to have low intelligence, to be incapable of making moral decisions and to be oriented toward the needs of the flesh.

The second image of women was epitomized by the Virgin Mary. In Catholicism, Mary was the mediator between God and humanity. It is she who takes on the devil, rebuking and punishing him with divine authority. Mary became a symbol of the chaste life, a state most pleasing to God. In this image women were perceived as holy and pure, completely devoid of sexuality. Mary also provided a feminine dimension for the divine. Prayer language in the Middle Ages, therefore, was more balanced between "male" and "female" metaphors. Julian of Norwich wrote that God was "as really our Mother as he is our Father."

In the midst of these conflicting views, it is not surprising that many women were attracted to the ascetic way of life. Asceticism permitted women to suppress their sexuality and strive towards holiness. Rather than restricting women, the development of monastic orders gave them new opportunities. They could live in community, escape the dangers of childbirth, and travel during religious pilgrimages.

Monastic life gave women the opportunity to develop leadership skills and exercise authority. In some places the abbess received the same recognition as abbots and bishops. She participated in parliaments, attended church councils, and signed official church decrees. She had jurisdiction over the clergy and lay people who lived on the land owned by the abbey and was answerable only to the Pope in Rome. Although she could not offer the sacraments, she gave spiritual guidance, heard confession, determined penance and gave absolution from sin. Some became quite powerful, such as Catherine Benincasa who exerted great influence over Pope Gregory and Urban VI.

The monastic life also gave women the opportunity to acquire great learning, and this in turn brought them to the attention of men in power. Melania the Younger taught theology to men and women. Marcella translated and interpreted Scripture. Lioba was trained in classical philosophy, theology, and canon law. Lioba (A.D. 779) was held in such high regard that Bishop Boniface asked her help in controlling the missionary churches in Germany.

By the eleventh and twelfth centuries the emphases of the monasteries changed to poverty and public preaching. Women attempting to open convents in conjunction with male monasteries often met resistance. Women were not thought capable of obeying the strict rules and attaining the level of perfection demanded by the orders. The Dominicans and Franciscans, who had encouraged the spiritual development of women, now resisted out of fear that they might have to support the women, and because association with women was still considered contaminating. In addition, women's freedom of movement was curtailed. Pope Boniface VIII tried to force the monastic women to stay in seclusion.

Some protested the church's restrictions on women. In the fifteenth century, Christiane de Pisan, a widow at the age of twenty-five, wrote against the attacks on women by medieval churchmen. She argued that "there was good evidence to show that many women were modest, gentle, and loving. As a group, they did not wage war, and they did not oppress other people. "Adam," she pointed out, "was just as guilty as Eve in bringing sin into the world. What is more, women were the ones who remained faithful to Jesus during his trial and death."

THE REFORMATION PERIOD

By Reformation times, sexuality was no longer seen as evil, and women were no longer viewed as temptresses and seducers. Both Luther and Calvin encouraged Christians, including priests, to marry. This gave some women a new sphere of opportunity as minister's wives. Their homes became centers of hospitality to theologians and theology students. Luther's wife, Katherine von Bora, worked with servants, children, visitors, students, theologians and church leaders.

According to Luther, men and women were equal in their responsibilities and privileges before the fall. He considered the subordination of women the result of Eve's sin. Calvin argued that woman was made after man as a "helper" for him—and that meant in subjection to him. Calvin felt that women had to be obedient to men. A wife was permitted to disobey her husband only when his commands caused her to disobey God. The reformers stressed that husbands were not to be cruel to their wives, but that if this did occur, women must be submissive. A woman could leave her husband only if her life was endangered.

The status of women was elevated by Luther and Calvin through a theology of motherhood as ordained by God. However, by removing the monastic life as an option for women, they restricted women's roles to those of motherhood and homemaking.

Based on their belief that the Bible taught the subordination of women, Lutherans and Calvinists generally did not allow women to preach, to be ordained, or to participate in the governing bodies of the churches. Luther did teach, however, that in unusual circumstances, when men were not available, a woman might preach as a temporary substitute.

Nevertheless, women were actively involved in spreading their faith. Sister Jeanne de Jussie, a nun in Geneva during the growth of Calvinism, writes of women's activities, including preaching, in spreading Calvinist doctrine. Jussie writes that the wife of an "apothecary" not only preached, but was regarded by Calvinist leaders as illuminated by God to teach and preach divine truth.

In summary, the Reformation opened the way for more participation by women in church affairs. While these activities were not encouraged in most churches, they did exist. And while women lost the monastery as a sphere of female autonomy, Reformation theology elevated the status of marriage and ended the association of women with evil. Girls were encouraged to attend school, specifically to learn to read the Bible; divorce laws protected women from abuse. Theologically, the stage was set for greater participation by women in church affairs by the emphasis on the priesthood of all believers.

ANABAPTIST WOMEN

Some sixteenth and seventeenth-century reform movements—Mennonites, Baptists, and Quakers—rejected the established connection between the church and state. Their belief in direct inspiration and individual freedom expressed itself in greater freedom for men and women in church ministries.

Women in these groups had more varied responsibilities than their Lutheran and Calvinist sisters and comprised a larger percentage of the congregations.

When these groups vested authority in the individual, and in the individual congregation, they opened the way for the participation of women.

The Quakers were the most open to the gifts of women but others also allowed some participation. English Separatist John Smyth gave women a vote in the selection of a pastor and the disciplining of members. Other leaders allowed women to speak to issues but not to vote. Some Mennonite churches in the Netherlands and North Germany revived the office of deacon for women, but the office was limited to widows over sixty. These deacons were not ordained, but in some cases were considered church officers. Others, such as Soetken Gerrits and Vrou Gerrits, wrote hymns.

Most early anabaptist groups held the traditional view of silence and subordination for women, but in practice women were seen as responsible and somewhat independent individuals. They were expected to make their own decisions regarding faith and practice. Many women died as martyrs for their faith. Religious incompatibility was added to adultery as grounds for divorce.

Opinion was mixed on whether or not women should preach. Most leaders taught the silence of women, but since anabaptist theology taught that the Holy Spirit could inspire any believer directly, regardless of education or gender, some women felt compelled to speak.

Women did exercise a preaching ministry in some congregations. Often they met with scorn and rebuke, occasionally for their teachings, but more often for their audacity. We have historical lists of women preachers highly regarded by their congregations, especially in Holland, France, and England. In one London congregation, hundreds of people regularly gathered on Tuesday afternoons to hear women preach.

In time the anabaptist groups became more institutionalized. They progressively conformed their practices to those of society and the established churches. As a result, the activities of women were curtailed, and the silence and subordination of women in the home and church was increasingly observed.

THE AMERICAN COLONIES

The image of woman as evil lingered on in the early years of the American colonies. Women were believed incapable of intellectual thought. Learning for women was regarded as inappropriate, even dangerous. Women were considered spiritually and morally weak, dishonest, and susceptible to heretical opinions. Because of such weaknesses, women were to be kept under control at all times. They were expected to be church members and attend worship regularly, but they generally did not vote and were discouraged from speaking in church meetings. In some congregations women were not allowed to sing in the worship service and were seated apart from the men. In those traditions where candidates for church membership were required to tell of their conversion, some ministers insisted that women do so privately. Since women were thought to be incapable of theological understanding, they were required to accept the explanations of male members or their husbands in matters of belief.

There are, however, examples of women prominent in American religious life. Anne Hutchinson was excommunicated for teaching that salvation is a personal relationship to Christ, and not related to "works." Anne

Eaton also was excommunicated for teaching adult baptism. Generally though, women had only minimal impact on Puritan theology and church life, and the trial of out-spoken women as witches greatly limited the freedom of women in the church.

Attitudes and practices were changing by the end of the seventeenth century. Men and women began to be regarded as spiritual equals. They had the same sinful natures and took the same journey to salvation. The prominent New England minister Cotton Mather wrote, "As a woman had the Disgrace to go first in that horrid and woeful transgression of our first Parents,...so a Woman had the Glory of bringing into the World that Second Adam, who is the Father of all our Happiness." In addition, their economic contributions on the farm and frontier became necessary for survival. While subordination continued to be taught, an emphasis on interdependence was closer to reality. More emphasis was put on love and mutuality in marriage, while also retaining the idea of subjection. This produced an interesting twist in theology. Women as submissive partners in a spiritual relationship became role models for all Christians. Women acquired a new status. Christians were encouraged to learn humility and receptiveness from the women in their congregations.

The great awakenings brought women new opportunities for service. Charles Finney allowed women to speak before mixed audiences. Although this aroused hostility among other evangelists, Finney continued the practice. He later became president of Oberlin College, which was the first college to admit women. (Antoinette Brown, the first woman to be ordained in the Congregational Church, was a graduate of Oberlin.) By the end of the eighteenth century, the Free Will

Baptists permitted women to serve as preachers and evangelists, joining the Quaker women serving as ministers and missionaries. These women played a significant part in spreading Christianity throughout the colonies.

THE NINETEENTH CENTURY

Developments in the field of psychology at the end of the eighteenth century changed views on the nature of women, and caused another shift in the role of women in American society and the churches. It became popular to believe that women were endowed with distinctly "feminine" characteristics. These qualities were then used to define the roles in which women would find happiness and which God had ordained for them. Women were said to be irrational, frail, emotional, intuitive, and nurturing. It was believed that because of these "feminine characteristics," women were more religious and moral than men, a very significant change from attitudes a century earlier. In addition to their homemaking responsibilities, women became responsible for protecting the faith and morality of society. Women were to accomplish this task through prayer and by teaching their sons to be God-fearing citizens.

Defining women by these "feminine characteristics" became very restrictive. Women who did not demonstrate these characteristics were considered masculine or interested in activities contrary to God's plan. While great damage was done by this strand of popular psychology, it opened new areas of participation within the Christian community.

By mid-century the concept of the ideal women as domestic, submissive, and pious was firmly planted in

the minds of white America. The American woman was
to find happiness at home in the role of wife and mother. At the same time, educational opportunities were
opening up for women. Without many career opportunities, many women were ripe for the development
of voluntary societies. Revival preachers emphasized
that conversion should be followed by good works, and
defined good works as active involvement in mission
and reform groups. Many of these groups worked to
raise money to support missionaries, to provide supplies
for mission work, or to meet the needs of women and
children at mission outposts. Women became very active
in these groups, and women's missionary societies soon
became an accepted part of church life.

These women's missionary societies also became the
context for challenge to the male domination of church
missions. Many groups were required to call in a male
minister to open their meetings with prayer or to give
an address. And women, while working hard for missions and contributing much money, were excluded from
the decision-making process of mission boards. Often,
the only option for a woman called by God to the mission
field was to marry a missionary, and even there her role
was that of wife and mother.

It became apparent that missionary work was ham-
pered because women were not actively involved. It was
impossible for male missionaries to reach women in
many cultures where women could only be spoken to or
approached by other women. Slowly mission boards began to send single women to the field.

Women began to form their own boards in the 1860's
rather than functioning as auxiliaries to denominational
boards. They raised their own funds, determined their
own policies, and sent women out as missionaries. These

boards made overseas mission work a possibility for large numbers of single women.

By the early part of the twentieth century, women represented two-thirds of the church's mission force. These women taught and managed schools, served in medical hospitals, published literature, led worship and preached. More than one modern missiologist has noted that the more difficult and dangerous the work, the higher the ratio of women to men. While meaningful ministry opportunities for women were restricted in North America, the opposite was true on the mission field. Every ministry was open to women. Lottie Moon sailed for China in 1873 as a school teacher. But she believed her gifts lay in evangelism and church planting. By the end of the century her work in P'ing-tu was described as "the greatest evangelistic center [among the Southern Baptists] in all China." The difference between what these women did on the mission field and the way they were treated when they returned to North America or Europe often became the source of great frustration. Malla Moe, an early TEAM missionary in Swaziland, functioned as the mission bishop, assigning pastors and overseeing their work. When she returned home, she was not permitted to speak in church.

The first major affirmation of women as preachers came from the holiness movement which developed out of the evangelical revivals. A high percentage of holiness ministers were women. The Church of the Nazarene affirmed the right of women to preach as early as 1894. Phoebe Palmer, a product of the holiness movement, preached as an evangelist in the United States, Canada and England. As a result of her ministry, Catherine Booth and Frances Willard felt God's call to public ministry. Booth and her husband, Willard, founded the

Salvation Army. Booth herself became an effective revival preacher and Willard, claiming that his best soldiers in urban missions were women, worked with Dwight Moody speaking on women's suffrage and temperance.

THE TWENTIETH CENTURY

Significant changes began to occur in the mainline Protestant churches at mid-century. The African Methodist Episcopal Church voted to ordain women in 1948. The United Methodist Church granted full conference rights (including preaching) to women in 1956. Also in 1956, the Presbyterian Church in the United States began to ordain women in keeping with its policy granting women full equality. The Presbyterian Church went a step further and refused to ordain men who were unable to recognize women as eligible for ministry. Seminaries opened all degree programs to women, no longer limiting them to studies in Christian Education or the status of "enrichment student."

Even with the admission of women to seminaries, ministry placements left much to be desired. Women were sent to less desirable churches. Their salaries were usually less than half the amount of men. Women, although professionally trained, were patronized, considered dispensable, and had poorly defined relationships with other church staff and with church councils. Women serving as ministers often became errand girls, burdened with the work male staff did not want.

Prompted by these concerns and the Civil Rights Act of 1964, which prohibited discrimination on the grounds of sex as well as race, many Christians, both women and

men, began to question the status of women in the
churches. Denominational reports and special studies
were prepared to deal with the issue from biblical and
practical perspectives. These studies made it apparent
that Christians were confronting deeply rooted traditions which affected the interpretation of Scripture.

The result was the formation of organizations within
denominational structures to promote equality for wom-
en. The American Baptist Convention formed its
Executive Staff Women in 1969 to study the involvement of women in the churches, and then followed
this up with a Task Force on Women. A United
Methodist Women's Caucus was established to promote
the rights and participation of women. The
Presbyterians organized a Council on Women and the
Church in 1973 to identify issues relevant to the status
of women in church and society. Also in 1973, the
Mennonite Central Committee established a Task Force
on Women's Concerns to promote new relationships and
corresponding supporting structures in which men and
women can grow toward wholeness and mutuality.

These councils advocate that churches continue to
strive for a greater participation of women on church
boards and councils, encourage women to train for the
ministry, and provide ministry opportunities for women
in the churches. They stress the importance of using inclusive language in worship, hymns, and church meetings. They also encourage women to dedicate themselves to the study of Scripture, church history, and
theology.

The past century has been one of great change in
North American churches. Evangelical preachers from
the period of the great awakenings began the process of
gently prodding women to use their God-given gifts and

talents. This movement, along with the societal changes in educational and economic opportunities for women, have encouraged them to participate more fully in the life and work of the church.

CONCLUSION

History suggests that new movements and churches that are focused outward in mission are more open to the ministry of women. When the church is in flux because of reform or when the church is overwhelmed by the work that needs to be done, it seems less concerned about who does what. As churches become institutionalized and turn inward toward maintenance, they tend to restrict the ministry of women. Nevertheless, the ministry of women in mission, both urban and foreign, has fueled the missionary outreach of the church in the modern world, and has produced some of the most outstanding leaders and results of the church in mission.

SUGGESTIONS FOR READING

Tucker, Ruth A., and Walter Liefeld. Daughters of the Church. Zondervan, 1987.

Tucker, Ruth A. Guardians of the Great Commission: The Story of Women in Modern Missions. Zondervan, 1988.

WOMEN IN THE MENNONITE BRETHREN CHURCH [1]

12

Katie Funk Wiebe

Images and Realities

Portion of a letter to the Area Administrative Office in Halbstadt, South Russia, in 1864, from the Molotschna Council of Church leaders explaining why they were unable to recognize the newly-formed Mennonite Brethren Church as a Mennonite Church:

"Since the secessionists have neither a church-ordained elder nor a properly appointed minister, and since they absolutely refuse to tie the teaching of the ministry of the church and the administration of the sacraments to an ecclesiastical office, but on the contrary have every member who feels called to do so administer these ordinances, — indeed, even the female members speak in their meetings and pray aloud — obviously in contradiction to 1 Cor. 12, 2 Cor. 5:18-20; James 3:1; 1 Cor. 14:34-35 and 1 Tim. 2:12 — therefore, according to the rules of our church, we can neither condone nor recognize as legal such unauthorized

1 For a longer documented version of this chapter, see <u>Mennonite Life</u> (September 1981), 22-28.

practices of theirs as baptism, communion and mar-
riage." P.M. Friesen adds an editorial comment that
the women spoke only in home gatherings. — P.M.
Friesen, The Mennonite Brotherhood in Russia 1789-
1910

In Shakespeare's "Twelfth Night," the duke asks
Viola about Olivia, whom he wants to marry: "And
what's her history?" Viola replies, "A blank, my lord."

To ask for the history of Mennonite Brethren women
is to receive the same answer. The record is a blank.
They have been given little room in the story of the
Mennonite Brethren church. History books offer little
help in revealing their role and contribution. Indexes of
such books have few entries under women's names.

It is true that women in the Mennonite Brethren
church have not been church leaders or contributors to
business, agriculture, and educational institutions in a
way openly visible to others and which made history.
Because their contribution is unrecorded, the assumption is sometimes made that women of the Mennonite
church in Russia, including the Mennonite Brethren,
which began there in 1860, were passive, uncreative,
unassertive, accepting their lot with equanimity.

Yet women have never been absent—only officially
unrecorded—and that has made them invisible to later
generations. They were present during the founding and
development of the Mennonite Brethren church, and
their early contribution can best be described as the
quiet shining of a lamp, rather than the powerful roar of
a waterfall.

What has been the particular contribution of women
to the founding of the Mennonite Brethren church and
thereafter? Their record is hidden between lines and in
footnotes, a story of women as human as that of their

husbands, brothers, and fathers. They, too, despaired, failed, sinned; they also were open to God's redemptive grace and overcoming love. They showed compassion for others, tenacity of spirit, and selfless endurance in the face of tremendous hardships. They were committed to Christ, his church, and its mission, inasmuch as social and religious limitations allowed them.

What Factors Contributed to Their Exclusion from History?

What factors, then, contributed to their official exclusion from history? One main reason is that archival material in historical libraries is not usually neatly catalogued under women's history, nor do researchers expect to find significant historical material under women's names when they do locate them.

Secondly, little in a historian's professional training equips him (and most historians have been men to date) to make sense of the lives of ordinary and powerless persons, particularly women, who were not part of the public record or who didn't openly influence church policies. Historians look for exceptional and powerful people and for the record of their influence in official minutes of public meetings, public debates, speeches, letters, and journals. The life stories of ordinary people who go about their daily tasks quietly and who do not see themselves as makers of history do not usually provide the material for history books.

In the case of the Mennonite Brethren church, additional factors that need to be considered are theology, language, and culture. A strong teaching in the Mennonite church in Russia was nonresistance, an issue which concerned primarily the sons in the family, not the daughters. Adherence to this doctrine determined whether or not the young men were drafted, and if they were, what type of service they would do in the military. Mennonite history often records fathers' concerns for sons who have to enter the army. Several Mennonite migrations occurred because of this concern for sons' welfare. Women—their needs and their role in relationship to the peace position—were not part of this major concern. Because the destiny of the Mennonites was wrapped up with the way sons were involved in this issue and not the way women experienced the truth of Scripture in relationship to it, women's contribution was not viewed as significant.

The ambivalent theology of the Mennonite Brethren with regard to women's roles in the church, particularly as it related to missions and ordination (see Ch. 11) has also made their contribution to the church an ambiguous or nonexistent one. Missionary service has always been an acceptable form of service for men or women from the beginning of the Mennonite Brethren church, even though in an overseas country, the woman, particularly if she was single, might engage in activities such as preaching, teaching, and leading an institution—activities not acceptable for woman to do in the home congregation.

In the early years of the Mennonite Brethren church, married couples and single women were encouraged to make a lifetime career of missions. All were ordained to such service, but the women were not officially allowed to preach. According to the Missionary Album, published in 1957, the Mennonite Brethren church ordained at least 85 women, 35 of them single women. Because the information is incomplete, the number is probably higher.

Paulina Foote, missionary to China for nineteen years, expresses some of her ambivalent feelings about the lack of clear direction regarding what a woman could or could not do overseas in the following excerpt from her memoirs written about her ordination in 1922 (God's Hand Over My Nineteen Years in China):

> The thought of an ordination gave me struggles. Women in our conference do not preach. Why should I be ordained if I could not proclaim the Gospel to those who had not heard it? Women were permitted to tell the Gospel to women and children. What if men would come to my women's and children's meetings? Should I stop proclaiming the Gospel message? Did not the men have a right to hear the Word of God? The church had asked Pastor Jacob Reimer of Bessie, Oklahoma, and Elder Johann Foth of the Ebenfeld Church near Hillsboro, Kansas, to officiate at my ordination. Both were considered to be of the most conservative in the whole conference. What a surprise to me when Elder Foth in his sermon at the ordination proved with Scripture passages that women should preach. He spoke about Mary Magdalene, who had followed Christ to the cross. . . She was the first of Christ's followers who was at the grave on the resurrection morning. She was the first to tell the greatest story of all stories that Christ had arisen from the dead. Christ Himself commanded her to carry the news to the disciples, the men, and to Peter who had failed Him. My problem about the ordination was solved. My later experience proved that this was of the Lord.

Though Miss Foote's mind was clear on the matter of her ordination, the church at home remained confused, and this ambivalence led to unclarity regarding what women who felt called to service in Christ's kingdom could do in the work of the church, both overseas and at home.

Not until 1957 did the General Conference of the Mennonite Brethren Church change its written policy regarding ordination of women to a commissioning, stating, "That in view of the fact that we as an M.B. Church, on the basis of clearly conceived Scriptural convictions, do not admit sisters to the public Gospel preaching ministry on par with brethren, we as Conference designate the fact of setting aside sisters to missionary work a 'commissioning' rather than an 'ordination.'" But the sluice gates could not be shut off with a conference resolution. Too many young women had been encouraged to listen for the call to missionary service and all that it might entail—and then later echoed Foote's frustrations.

Another reason for the invisibility of women in Mennonite Brethren history is a misunderstanding of the Russian Mennonite culture that cradled the Mennonite Brethren church. We read Mennonite Brethren church history with North American eyes. We count church membership here by persons; two hundred names means two hundred members. The situation in South Russia at the time of the founding of the Mennonite Brethren church was a little different. In that culture, which was introduced from Prussia, a son or daughter belonged to the father's family until marriage, when a new family unit was set up in the village books. Land was apportioned to family units, not to individuals. As soon as a son or daughter married, his or her name was taken off the parental family register and together with the spouse considered as a new unit. People migrated as family units and were processed as family units, often with widowed members, foster children, and even servants as part of the group. In church life, the same system prevailed.

Alan Peters of Fresno, California, has done much research showing how the signers of the Document of

Secession of the Mennonite Brethren Church in 1860 were mostly young men, many related through their wives, and how the family contributed significantly to the development of the early Mennonite Brethren church. Yet, today, when modern readers see 18 signatures attached to the Document of Secession, some deduct that these 18 names represent 18 individuals rather than 18 family heads representing 18 family units, a much different number. Eighteen men signed the document, but the charter membership consisted of about 54 people, according to P. M. Friesen. Historians who state that the church was begun by "eighteen men" read into Friesen something he never intended to say.

Friesen writes that in the fall of 1859, two weeks after St. Martin's, a few *Geschwister* (usually translated brothers and sisters) were gathered in one of the member's homes for the Lord's Supper. As a result, these members were placed under the ban, and later excommunicated and civilly ostracized. On January 6, 1860, the Founding Document was signed by 18 heads of families and a little later by nine others. Peter Regier, in his short history, states that women were present at this meeting but did not sign. Jakob Reimer and other Gnadenfeld members who signed with him agreed that on January 6, 1860, the Mennonite Brethren church began. Yet in a footnote, historian Friesen explains that the 18 plus 9, or 27, refers to 27 heads of families and denotes men of full age and a corresponding number of sisters. Johann Claassen, early leader, in a writing to the Czar, dated May 21, 1862, states the number of Mennonites involved in the January 6, 1860, event to be "ca. 50." In another footnote dealing with Claassen's reference to the January 6, 1860, meeting, Friesen explains again, "The members of the family and sympathizers are included with the 18 family heads who united on January 6, 1860, to sign the important document." He refers to his mother and his eldest sisters as members of Bible study groups and charter sisters of the Mennonite Brethren church, together with the men. Clearly, a better understanding of the cultural context would have kept writers from making the mistake of attributing the founding of the church to only 18 men.

Another factor making the women invisible and therefore also their contribution, is the German language, which makes it possible to use a term like *Geschwister*, which can mean brothers and sisters, or only brothers, or only sisters, and male-oriented language like *Brueder* (brethren) generically. This terminology, now considered exclusive, was used out of a desire for greater intimacy and warmth among the early leaders, but gradually shut out the majority of the church—the women.

Women's Contribution to the Mennonite Brethren Church

Despite such factors, women made a significant contribution to the founding and growth of the Mennonite Brethren church.

1. Women strongly supported their husbands in their open decisions and quietly influenced the direction their lives were taking. Friesen mentions repeatedly Johann Claassen's high regard for his wife, Katharina, to whom he entrusted important information about legal matters of the early church. He also entrusted her to undertake certain actions on his behalf in his absence, not customary for women in those times. Elizabeth Suderman Klaassen in Trailblazer for the Brethren has enlarged on Katharina Claassen's contribution to the

development of the Mennonite Brethren church in this biography.

Jakob Reimer, another of the leaders, had a high regard for women and mentions them frequently in his writings. He states he was influenced theologically, especially with regard to baptism, by Anne Judson, wife of Baptist missionary Adoniram Judson, with the result that the first baptism performed by the secessionists used the form of immersion.

Historian P.M. Friesen also had a high regard for women and mentions them freely. He writes that the determining influences on his life were his mother and eldest sister, charter members of the church. He credits his wife with being his "best secretary" as he worked with five thousand pages of manuscript. According to A.A. Vogt's index of persons named in Friesen's history, 97 women are mentioned, most of them either teachers, missionaries, or wives of church workers. Not all, of course, are Mennonite Brethren. By contrast J.H. Lohrenz's The Mennonite Brethren Church includes no women in the biographical section and J.A. Toews's A History of the Mennonite Brethren Church lists only nine women in the index.

2. A second major contribution by women was their gift of hospitality. "Share with God's people who are in need. Practice hospitality" writes the author of Romans, after discussing the gifts of the Spirit (Rom. 12). Because the Mennonite Brethren had no meeting houses of their own at first, all services were held in homes. Traveling ministers and their families, some of whom were fleeing or moving to other areas to escape harassment, found refuge in homes. Because at first the Mennonite Brethren church was a house (home) or small group movement, and few houses were very large,

women will have been much aware of what was happening and more involved than at first seems apparent.

3. According to historian Cornelius Krahn, "The emphasis on spontaneous conversion and antipathy toward tradition broke barriers and promoted equality in general, and also between the sexes. Paul's admonition, 'Let the women be silent in the churches,' (1 Cor. 14:34) was interpreted to mean only that women should not preach" in the early Mennonite Brethren church. "With the introduction of Bible study, prayer meeting, Sunday school, and mission societies, a wide field was opened for women. Now they could express their views in Bible studies, they participated audibly in prayer meetings, they taught Sunday school classes, discussed missionary affairs in sewing circles and many other organizations, and as mission workers engaged in direct evangelism and teaching."

A close reading of Friesen's history supports Krahn's views of the status of women in the Mennonite Brethren church. They contributed by taking part in the singing, prayers, testimonies, and discussion of Bible passages. Friesen reports that the Kuban church, formed later on, was especially blessed with vital and pious praying sisters. He adds, somewhat humorously, "Day and night one could undoubtedly say, there was always a priest in the holy place . . . even though it was a priestess, according to the New Testament pattern: 'There is neither male nor female, for you are all one in Christ Jesus' (Gal. 3:28)." Obviously, he delighted in the role reversals. Women were converted, baptized, and received into membership, but also excommunicated during time of emotional excesses.

The question of how much they actually participated in the more formal meetings is not clear, although it is possible to make assumptions similar to Krahn's views. It is also not clear from the Friesen account whether women participated in annual brotherhood consultations or conventions as the church grew. By 1879, sixteen years after the church was founded, the General Conference of Mennonite Brethren Churches in America decided this issue by agreeing that "sisters may take part in church activities as the Holy Spirit leads. However, they should not preach or take part in discussion meetings of the church." At the same convention the continuing participation of women in mission work was affirmed.

4. In addition to considerable participation in church life during the early years, women had two other ties with the church, although neither was a policy-making role. As already mentioned, women were encouraged to become missionaries. They also became members of sewing societies in their home congregations primarily to support missions. These women's groups were transplanted to America from Russia and here underwent various transformations, sometimes functioning as an auxiliary to the church and later on sometimes almost as a church in themselves, operating almost parallel to the congregation with its own budget, aggressive program, membership list, and annual meetings and retreats. These women's groups have become a significant part of a caring ministry in the church for missionary families, for overseas nationals, especially women and children in recent decades.

Friesen mentions that Mennonites generally were recognized for their sacrificial donations of money, services, and products, including clothing, bedding, and bandages as the need arose during the war years in Russia, including the Crimean war, all of which activities will have involved women. Women are mentioned in the literature of the famine years in South Russia, following the Russian Revolution, as setting out food for beggars, of carrying food to a starving neighbor, of caring for the sick—their own and that of the enemy anarchists. This role of caring for the needy in good times and bad was expected of them, but because it was not institutionalized, the official record of their contribution is often missing.

5. The gift of women's suffering for their faith in Russia has not been recognized to the same extent as it was during anabaptist times when women were persecuted for their faith just like the men. Martyrs' Mirror includes stories of many such women as does the small book Geschichte der Maertyrer, which covers the stories of early Mennonite martyrs to about 1782 and lists at least one-third women. A.A. Toews' Mennonitische Maertyrer by contrast mentions only one woman by name in the index together with her husband and an entry "women martyrs" about three pages long.

Yet a careful study of this book reveals that when men were imprisoned, conscripted, exiled, women remained at home and endured, clinging to the faith, cherishing it, and nurturing it so that when times improved, the church could again pick up its mission. Because they were living on the underside of history as wives, sisters, and mothers, and men were in the public sphere as church leaders, their stories were omitted or given glancing notice. Paradoxically, women wrote many of the accounts in Toews' book of their husbands' suffering.

Overseas workers in missions or in Mennonite Central Committee service frequently mention that the bottom line of suffering in Third World countries is always the suffering of women. When there isn't enough food, women are the last to eat. When there isn't enough work, women are the first to be out of work. When there isn't enough room at school or enough money for fees, girls are the first to stay home. It is true, however, that when the church is persecuted, men, particularly church leaders, are often the first to be affected, nor should anyone deny their suffering as other than real, intense, and tragic. But the suffering of the women left behind to care for the family's total needs, to deal with the mental and emotional anguish because of the absence of loved ones, sometimes physically abused, sexually assaulted, and also exiled, imprisoned, or murdered, is equally real, intense, and tragic. It deserves at least a nodding recognition in view of the fact that without these women's will to trust a sovereign God who allowed such suffering, the church would have ceased to exist.

Stories are recorded of how, during the trek from the Ukraine to Poland and Germany following World War 2, a trek composed mostly of women, children, and older or sickly men, when people died or were killed by bombing attacks, women spoke a hymn and said the final prayer before the shallow grave was closed.

During the years when groups of Mennonite believers living in Siberia and Asiatic Russia were without spiritual leadership, women arranged meetings, read the Bible, and sang hymns, write A. and K. Plett and M. Peters in A Wilderness Journey: Glimpses of the Mennonite Brethren Church in Russia 1925-1980. These women's faith gleamed in that dark period like the quiet shining of a lamp, lighting the way for the next generation. Women kept the faith and modeled the Christian life in faithfulness to God during one of the most difficult periods of Mennonite history.

Mennonite Brethren Women in North America

At one time women were excluded from congregational business meetings in North American congregations. They couldn't vote. They couldn't even listen in. Then, in 1879, someone at a General Conference convention asked: "How do we feel about sisters attending such meetings?"

The delegates decided "the sisters could take part in the services as God's Spirit led them, but not to hold a teaching position and to keep silent in brotherhood deliberations." Each church should decide whether or not women could vote for a teaching minister or elder. Today I know of no congregation where women are not allowed such participation.

Involvement in conference decision-making structures also came slowly— but it did come. Women have long been present at conferences as silent observers— usually in the back left corner of the auditoriums and in the basement preparing the meals. The women usually ate at a second setting, after the male delegates had eaten. They discussed issues with their husbands at home. Today both single and married women attend church conventions in increasing numbers as delegates and visitors. Some conferences even provide food services and child care, freeing women to attend all sessions.

About the turn of the century the General Conference Mennonite Church under the leadership of David Goertz began a deaconess training school in Newton, Kansas, to develop single women's innate skills and give them an opportunity for Christian service. The first motherhouse was established in Newton under the direction of Sister Frieda Kaufman.

In exchange for vows of celibacy, poverty, and obedience for as long as the woman believed the diaconate was her place of service, the diaconate promised her lifetime support, opportunity for service, and blessed her ministry with ordination. Women from other branches of the Mennonite church, including Krimmer Mennonite Brethren and Mennonite Brethren, attended the school in Newton as well as elsewhere before these schools closed their doors in the late 1950s and 1960s.

Today women are attending seminary, earlier an almost entirely male institution, in increasing numbers. Women are also involved in teaching Bible classes for both women's and mixed classes.

Although deacons used to be male, today husband-and-wife teams are being chosen, and occasionally a woman (married or single) is called to this important ministry on the basis of her own gifts. Wives are being included as an important member of a pastoral couple, although their role is not always clear.

Representation of women in local congregational and conference structures has come slowly, although a few women are being elected to local church as well as conference committees and boards.

In some congregations women function as choir leader, song leader, church moderator, and in youth ministries, and occasionally preach on Sunday mornings. In a number of congregations in the United States and Canada, a woman is a member of the full-time pastoral staff in some capacity.

The story is obviously not yet complete. Some day when another history of the Mennonite Brethren church is written, may it include, along with the public church statements and decisions, the private personal history of its women, the domestic history of the family, the way in which male-controlled institutions have affected women's and men's lives, and how the consciousness grew in the Mennonite Brethren church that God has given spiritual gifts to both men and women for all types of service.

Such a history will require reading between the lines, perusing journals and memoirs, and perhaps reading with a woman's eyes and emotions to recreate the kinds of persons these early women were and how they contributed to the growth of the church. The setting for their early contribution has rarely been in the open, in full view of congregations or church councils, but by the hearth and by the lamp; and when the hearth was cold, and the light nearly gone, it was in the darkness, waiting for a new day to dawn for themselves, their families, and the church.

SUGGESTIONS FOR READING

Bekker, Jacob P. Origin of the Mennonite Brethren Church. Trans. by D.E. Pauls and A.E. Janzen. Mennonite Brethren Historical Society of the Midwest, 1973.

Foote, Paulina. God's Hand over My Nineteen Years in China. Mennonite Brethren Publishing House, 1962.

Friesen, P.M. The Mennonite Brotherhood in Russia (1789-1910). Trans. by J.B. Toews et. al. Board of Christian Literature, 1978.

Geschichte der Maertyrer oder kurze historische Nachricht von den Verfolgungen der Mennoniten. Mennonitischen Gemeinden Manitobas, 1938.

Janzen, A.E. and Herbert Giesbrecht. We Recommend . . . Recommendations and Resolutions of the General Conference of the Mennonite Brethren Churches. Board of Christian Literature, 1978.

Klassen, Elizabeth Suderman. Trailblazers for the Brethren. Herald Press, 1978.

Lohrenz, John H. The Mennonite Brethren Church. Board of Foreign Missions, 1950.

"Mennonite Brethren Church." Mennonite Encyclopedia. Mennonite Publishing House, 1959.

Peters, Alan. "Brotherhood and Family: Implications of Kinship in Mennonite Brethren History." P.M. Friesen and His History: Perspectives on Mennonite Life and Thought, No. 2. Center for Mennonite Brethren Studies, 1979.

Toews, A.A., ed. Mennonitische Maertyrer der Juengsten Vergangenheit unter der Gegenwart. Self-published, 1949.

Wiebe, Katie Funk. Our Lamps were Lit: An Informal History of the Bethel Deaconess Hospital School of Nursing. Bethel Hospital School of Nursing Alumnae Association, 1978.

_____. Women Among the Brethren: Stories of Fifteen Mennonite Brethren and Krimmer Mennonite Brethren Women. Board of Christian Literature, 1979.

Woelk, Heinrich and Gerhard Woelk. A Wilderness Journey: Glimpses of the Mennonite Brethren Church in Russia 1925 - 1980. Center for Mennonite Brethren Studies, 1982.

John E. Toews
Valerie Rempel

Summary and Implications

What Is the Discussion About?

Two interpretations are put forward in this book. The first says there is a permanent and normative creation order that establishes the headship of men over women, or that gives men the lead responsibility in church ministries. It argues that this creation order was instituted by God at creation. It finds confirmation in the rest of the Old Testament in the patriarchal structure of family and community life in Israel, and by the restriction of the priesthood to men. According to this interpretation, redemption in Christ does not reverse creation order. It consistently reads the New Testament texts that deal with church leadership and family relations (1 Cor. 12 and 14, 1 Tim. 2 and Eph. 4) as using creation order to limit the roles and ministries of women.

This first interpretation views men and women as equal in creation and redemption, but understands creation order to differentiate levels of responsibility for each. These differentiated responsibilities place boundaries on the roles of women. Women are gifted for ministry just as men are, but the public exercise of their ministries must occur within the context of male leadership. The critical issue regarding the ministry of women is not giftedness, but differentiated gender roles which limit certain ministries of women.

The second interpretation asserts the equality and complementarity of men and women, and the full gifting of women for church ministry. This interpretation is based on four biblical teachings.

First, man and woman together represent the image of God in creation (Ch. 4). Man and woman are equal and different. The differentness is viewed as complementary. This view argues that the creation accounts do not teach the subordination of woman to man. It notes that man does not name woman—the classic symbol of subordination—until after the fall. It does not read disapproval of women in leadership, even though such leadership is rare (Ch. 5), nor does it understand the Old Testament to teach the subordination of women based on creation.

Secondly, the teaching and practice of Christ underscore the equality of men and women (Ch. 6). Jesus and the gospels reject sexual discrimination and eliminate role differences based on gender.

Thirdly, salvation and baptism wipe out the sexual differences that divide and alienate non-Christian people and societies (Ch. 7). In Christ all people are equal in terms of salvation and relations in the church. The social consequences of baptism into the church are equality; thus sexually determined church roles are ended in Christ.

The fourth biblical teaching emphasizes the importance of gifting by the Spirit for the ministry of men and women (Chs. 8, 10). Women are gifted for leadership in the church and exercise their gifts in the early church.

The second interpretation reads the restrictive texts as important to maintain sexual identity in the church, and marriage and family commitments (1 Cor. 11, 14, 1 Tim. 2). The 1 Timothy 2 text either is an historically time-specific instruction for the church in Ephesus that cannot be universalized, or a text that again addresses husband/wife relationships rather then church leadership in public worship. Likewise, the Ephesians 5 text concerns family relationships, not church leadership issues.

The two interpretations agree on several important points. First, men and women are equal as persons in creation and redemption. Second, women are gifted for ministry and should be freed and empowered by the church to exercise their ministries.

The two interpretations differ only at one critical point. The one says that women must exercise their gifts under male leadership. The second says women are free to exercise their gifts independently and interdependently with men as equals. The first argues for hierarchical relationships between men and women in church leadership; the second argues for the liberation of men and women from hierarchical relationships in church leadership. The critical issue that divides the two interpretations is the meaning of "creation order" and "headship."

How Do We Interpret the Bible?

We have two different interpretations of the same biblical texts in this book. Both interpretations are made by people equally committed to the full inspiration and authority of the Bible, and both are based on a careful reading of the Bible. How can this be? How can the teachers of the church disagree on biblical interpretation? Such disagreements are a result of several factors.

First, we are dealing with different texts written at different times in history to address different issues in the life of different believing communities, Israel and the church. There is Genesis 1 and 2, there are the words of Jesus, and there are the writings of Paul. The latter represent the biggest problem. Paul says things that directly affirm women in ministry, e.g., Romans 16:1-16 (women are identified as leaders, apostles and co-workers), 1 Corinthians 11:2-16 (women pray and prophesy publicly, gender differences "in Christ" are irrelevant), Galatians 3:28 (baptism erases social differences based on gender in the church), Philippians 4:2-3 (women are leaders in the church), and 1 Timothy 5:3-16 (an "order" of widows serves the church). But Paul also restricts the public role of women, e.g., 1 Corinthians 14:33b-36 (women are not to ask questions in church), and 1 Timothy 2:8-15 (women are to learn quietly, and are not permitted to usurp authority from men). The problem is intensified by the use of words and grammar that can have more than one meaning, for example, the naming of Eve, the meaning of *kephale* ("head"), and *authentein* ("authority"). The same text can be interpreted differently depending on which definition an interpreter chooses.

Secondly, we are dealing with different interpreters. Every interpreter brings a pre-understanding or bias to the text. There is no such thing as "objective interpretation." Gender, race, class, nationality, religious experience, marital status and experience, power status, and many other historical and cultural realities, influence how each person interprets the text. Thus different interpreters interpret the same texts, even the same words, differently.

Such interpretive diversity is not new. It has characterized the history of the church. Most theological disagreements in the church are the result of equally committed believers interpreting the biblical text differently.

The diversity in this book reflects the diversity of text and interpreter. Elmer Martens and Allen Guenther disagree on the interpretation of Genesis 1 and 2. Martens gives priority to Genesis 2, while Guenther gives priority to Genesis 1. Martens thinks the naming of Eve reflects a "creation order" hierarchy of relationships, Guenther says the passive form of the "naming" word only characterizes and does not order. Guenther argues that since Adam's naming of Eve comes after the fall, it reflects the hierarchy of sin rather than of creation. Elmer Martens disagrees with John E. Toews on the meaning of *kephale* ("head") and the significance of "creation order" in the New Testament. These are honest differences between equally committed interpreters of the Bible, and in this case among friends and colleagues in the same church and in the same seminary of the church.

Differences of biblical interpretation are a normal part of church life. They always have been, and they always will be. The question is, how do we sort out which of these interpretations is preferable?

One common approach says the critical guideline is the starting point of diverse texts. This principle usually says that priority should be given to the clear texts. Genesis 1 is clear, but Genesis 2 involves a host of interpretive issues and problems. One group argues that Galatians 3:28 is the starting point for understanding Paul. Others insist that 1 Timothy 2:11-15 is the clearest of the Pauline texts, and should be the "window" for understanding the other Pauline texts. There is, of course, nothing in the Bible itself which tells us which texts should be given priority. That decision already reflects the bias we bring to the text. The issue of which text is the clearer is itself a controversial matter. The 1 Timothy 2 text is filled with serious, and in some cases unresolvable, difficulties (see Ch. 10 for details). On strictly exegetical grounds the Genesis 1 and Galatians 3 texts are much clearer texts. But that is not the main point of this section. It is, rather, that the question of which text we use as a starting point is itself an open question; the Bible itself gives no guidance on that question.

A second, and theologically more fruitful principle, says that differing texts must be ordered on the basis of which expresses the essence of the gospel most clearly. Two approaches may be used.

The first approach starts with Jesus. Jesus is understood to be the norm for ordering conflicting texts. Everyone is agreed that Jesus' relationships with women were revolutionary. Susan Foh, a conservative evangelical, and Mary Daly, a post-Christian feminist, are agreed that what Jesus did with and for women should change once and for all the way the church and the western world views and treats women (see Foh, 90-94, Daly, 79-80). On the basis of this principle, the liberating Pauline texts are given priority over the more restrictive texts.

The second approach starts with the theological essence of the gospel. The gospel of grace, forgiveness, and freedom is the starting point. Thus F.F. Bruce argues that the Pauline texts which liberate women for ministry are closest to the intention of Paul. The restrictive texts are examples of adaptation for a specific time and setting, and must not be normative for other times and places (see Gasque).

The attempt to order the relationship of texts on the basis of the essence of the gospel introduces a profound theological issue. Such ordering distinguishes between the authority of the text and its normativeness. The whole Bible is authoritative. But the text functions differently in different times and places. For example, the command to "greet one another with a holy kiss" is authoritative (it is commanded 5 times—Rom. 16:16; 1 Cor. 16:20; 2 Cor. 13:12; 1 Thes. 5:26; 1 Pet. 5:14—in the NT), but it is not practiced today because times have changed. People greet each other differently today than in the first century. Paul's command for women to wear a head covering is no longer expected because times have changed. Paul's restrictive words in 1 Corinthians 14 and 1 Timothy 2 are authoritative. Are they normative today? Or, have the specific occasions which called forth those instructions changed? These are questions on which equally committed evangelical people disagree. The point of disagreement is not the authority, or even the interpretation, of the text, but the applicability of a specific text in our time.

Is There a Permanent Creation Order?

One of the critical points of disagreement in the two interpretations of this book is the status of "creation order." Elmer Martens sees a permanent and normative creation order—male headship over women instituted by God in the creation accounts—that necessitates male leadership over women in the home and in the church. The other writers do not see such a permanent creation order. Allen Guenther reads the creation accounts to underline the equality and complementarity of men and women. Gordon and Lorraine Matties disagree that the Old Testament uses creation order or the fall (Gen. 3) to subordinate women.

What about the New Testament? The creation accounts are used four times in the New Testament. Jesus uses Genesis 1:27—God made humanity male and female—and 2:24—a man is to leave father and mother and become one flesh with his wife—to reject divorce. The text says nothing about a creation hierarchy or about the subordination of woman to man, only that a man is to leave his parental home and become genuinely one with his wife. The problem seems to lie with the man, not the woman.

Paul uses Genesis 1:27 in 1 Corinthians 11 to argue the necessity of a head covering for women in the church and to underline the interdependence of men and women. Again, there is no talk of hierarchy or subordination of women to men. The only issue is proper dress for women in public ministry. Genesis 2:24 is used in Ephesians 5 to command husbands to love their wives as Christ loved the church, not to exhort wives to be submissive to their husbands. There is no hierarchy; mutual submission is asked of both the wife and the husband. 1 Timothy 2 uses Genesis 2:7 and 22 to explain why women should learn quietly (the only command in the text), and why Paul does not permit wives to sexually seduce or manipulate their husbands as part of their teaching. Hierarchical relations and submission language is not used in the text.

Old and New Testament usage raises serious questions about any kind of creation order. Such an order is certainly not explicit in any text. And where creation accounts are used in the New Testament, they are used primarily to exhort men, not women.

What Is the Meaning of Headship?

A second matter of common disagreement is the meaning of "headship." Some interpreters argue that headship clearly teaches a hierarchical relationship between men and women in the home and in the church, and the necessity of women to submit to men in the home and in the church. The problem is whether the meaning of *kephale* ("head") in Greek is "source" or "chief."

In the English language "head" usually means the one with authority over others. But in Greek the meaning is not that simple. The most comprehensive dictionary of the Greek language lists over twenty possible meanings for *kephale*. The primary meaning has to do with source or origin. Although possible, the use of *kephale* to mean "chief" or "the person of highest rank" is very rare in Greek. The point is that *kephale* has multiple meanings.

The meaning in any particular text must be determined by the context, including the other words used in association with it. The only texts in the women in ministry discussion that use *kephale* are 1 Corinthians 11 and Ephesians 5 (see Chs. 8 and 9 for details). The word is not used in 1 Corinthians 14 or 1 Timothy 2. Most commentators agree that in 1 Corinthians 11 it means source; its meaning is defined by the creation reference in vv. 8-9 which speak of man as the source of woman and woman as the source of man. Ephesians 5 uses it to describe the relationship of the wife to the husband. The husband is characterized as the head of the wife. What follows makes it clear that this headship does not mean authority over, but rather service under. For the husband to be the head of the wife means to love her, not to subordinate her.

The New Testament clearly uses headship language, but not to argue for a hierarchical relationship between men and women or to make the case for the subordination of women to men. Headship means men and women are the source of each other's lives, and that men are to love their wives.

The authors of this chapter believe that neither creation order nor headship as a hierarchical structure can be used to argue that women may exercise their gifts (the point on which all authors are agreed) only under the leadership of men (the only point on which the authors disagree). We believe the evidence favors the full equality of men and women in creation, redemption and ministry, and therefore, frees women to exercise the gifts of ministry given them by the Holy Spirit for the upbuilding of the church.

Why Are There No Clear Examples of Women Ministering in the New Testament?

The question asked most often is, if the preceding interpretation of freedom for ministry is correct, why doesn't the New Testament give us examples of women ministering in the early church? We think it does.

Acts reports that four daughters of the evangelist Philip prophesied in the church. Romans 16 reports nine women in important roles in the mission and life of the Roman congregation. Phoebe is a deaconness and a patron of the church at Cenchreae. In addition, Paul identifies a series of other female co-workers: Prisca (vv. 3-5), Mary (v. 6), Junia, an apostle (v. 7), Tryphaena, Tryphosa, Persis, Julia and Nereus' sister (vv. 12-15). 1 Corinthians adds Chloe and Philippians names Euodia and Syntyche (see Chs. 2, 7, 10).

The fact that women are singled out in letters written by Paul to whole congregations suggests that they held leadership positions. What emerges from these names is a clear picture of women who worked at the center of the Pauline mission and congregational life.

One other example is worth noting. 2 John begins with "the elder to the elect lady and her children, whom I love in the truth." Some commentators suggest the "elect lady" means the church, but the simplest and most obvious reading is that the woman was the leader of the "house church" and the "children" were the Christians who met in her home (John often calls believers "children," e.g., 1 Jn. 2:1, 3:18, 5:2, 21, and 3 Jn. 4).

Why Now?

Even if the above were true, why does the call for the affirmation of women in ministry come at this time? Is the church not simply absorbing the ideas of secular feminism? Is the church not being conformed to the culture?

In part, the answer is yes. The church is always influenced by the prevailing culture. There can be no doubt that the feminist movement in the Western world has influenced us in the church, just as secular capitalist ideas have deeply shaped thought and life in the church. Ironically, there is scholarship which suggests that the feminist movement also owes much to evangelical women who formed the heart of the missionary movement during the late 19th and early 20th centuries. Larger cultural movements have always influenced the church, and taught the church to read the Bible through new eyes. But this explanation is too superficial. There are other, deeper forces of change at work in our culture.

Feminism is part of a much larger pattern of change in Western society. At one time people were assigned roles in life based on forces outside of their control, such as class, religion, race, gender, ethnic identity, marital status and geographic location. Some were farmers because that is what their parents were; others were merchants, or teachers, or servants. This has changed in the modern West. Today, roles are much more a matter of choice and ability. We no longer ask who a person's parents were or on what side of the tracks the person lived, but whether the person is competent for the job or role he or she undertakes. Most of us are grateful for this change. We are immensely thankful that even though our parents were poor, or uneducated, we now can become business persons, schoolteachers, university professors, health care professionals, lawyers, or pastors. But in the church we often forget that the movement away from ascribed roles cannot be neatly cut off at a certain point. The very people who greatly benefit from new opportunities cannot suddenly say they are not open to women in the church. We need to realize that we are dealing with a large social pattern that most of us support most of the time.

Two areas have become the focus of controversy in the West: race and gender. Today almost everyone in North American society agrees that people should not be forbidden certain roles because of race, and most people say the same should be true for gender. Yet some in the church want to say that because of gender, certain persons should be restricted in the exercise of God-given gifts. Even if the movement of feminism disappeared, the pressure for gender inclusiveness would continue to build in the church. Why? Because we are dealing with a larger social pattern that cannot be arbitrarily cut off. Women now enjoy the benefits of education, both secular and theological. They read their Bibles and learn for themselves the message of God's justice and liberation. They experience the gifting of the Holy Spirit for ministry. They hear and respond affirmatively to the call of God to exercise their gifts. But too often, they discover that the church refuses to let them exercise their gifts (usually while denying that it has), and refuses to acknowledge that they have received a call from God (again while denying that it has), simply because they are women. Many men and women are asking, why? The question raised is one of justice. People are asking why gender is relevant when God gives gifts of ministry. Clearly the gifts of the Spirit are relevant, but why gender?

The old answer that "this is how God wants it" no longer works. Women can read and interpret the Bible themselves. They know that many biblical passages affirm their ministry, and that the traditionally restrictive texts are problematic at multiple levels. Furthermore, they have heard the church say that men and women are spiritually equal. They are aware that the church has blessed the significant contributions of women in overseas mission fields and parachurch organizations. Many women and men can no longer accept the idea that all are spiritually equal, but that in the ministries of the local church they are unequal.

There was a time, especially during the last century and the early part of this century, when the church responded much more positively to the decline of gender-based roles. Women were much freer to minister and to lead in the church from the seventeenth through the early part of the twentieth century. The Protestant Reformation's break with the Catholic concept of the minister as priest, based on the Old Testament priesthood, had liberating consequences for the ministry of women. John Calvin believed that the freedom of women to minister was a matter of human opinion based on particular cultures rather than a clear teaching of Scripture. Free church traditions, especially Anabaptist and Quaker, gave women special opportunity to minister in the sixteenth and seventeenth centuries. A good number of women can be identified as ministers among the Baptists in Holland, England and America. The theological ground for this acceptance was an understanding that the Spirit empowers both men and women for ministry. The Wesley revivals in the eighteenth century encouraged both lay men and women to preach and minister. The same occurred in the eighteenth-century Great Awakening in America and the Evangelical Awakening in the nineteenth century. The revivalists stressed the importance of personal experience with God as a criterion for ministry. Many women responded. In fact, women were often viewed as more religious and spiritual than men in a theology of "true womanhood" that developed during this century.

In addition, women were given new educational opportunities. As they studied the Bible on their own they felt increasingly called by God into church ministries. They moved to the vanguard of the anti-slavery and revival movements. The more they worked for the freedom of blacks, in part on the basis of texts like Galatians 3:28, the more they recognized their own equality and freedom in Christ.

The nineteenth century became known as the age of woman preachers. Three of the great preachers of the century were Phoebe Palmer, a Methodist evangelist and revivalist, Catherine Booth, founder of the Salvation Army, and Hannah Whithall Smith, one of the key founders of the Keswick Conference. Many denominations—Free Will Baptists, Free Methodists, Quakers, Brethren Church, Christian Missionary Alliance, the Church of God (Anderson, Ind.), the Church of God (Cleveland), Evangelical Free Church, Church of the Nazarene, American Baptists, and various Pentecostal groups—affirmed, even ordained, women for ministry.

All of this changed in the 1920s. The evangelical movement of the post-World War I era became restrictive on the question of women in ministry (see Ch. 12, and the article by Gloria Redekop for the same pattern in the Mennonite Brethren Church). An affirmation and openness for ministry that was experienced theologically and practically throughout the nineteenth century suddenly became a problem. Women were now told that they were excluded from ministry because of their gender.

Most women in evangelical American churches endured the post-1920 restrictions patiently, though painfully, until the 1950s. However, the evangelical renaissance of the 1950s included a growing desire and calling by women to exercise the gifts of the Spirit in the church. That desire has increased with the rejection of ascribed gender roles in the West. Today this growing desire has become a loud crescendo calling for true biblical justice and the freedom to exercise the gifts and the call the Spirit gives to the church.

Why now? First, because the inner structure and the basic values of western culture are changing. Roles based on ascribed characteristics are being replaced by roles based on choice and competence. These changes came about because of the teachings and activities of the church in proclaiming the gospel over the centuries. Secondly, because the church has become more restrictive since 1920. Consequently, the cries of pain from women gifted for ministry have become louder and the calls for change more strident. If certain forms of ministry by women created problems in the culture of the Pauline churches (note the honor and shame language used in 1 Corinthians 14 and 1 Timothy 2), the opposite is true today. In our day, insisting on the silence of women in the church brings shame on the church.

What Shall We Do in the Church?

We live between the times on many issues in the church. The role of women in church ministry is one of these issues. What, then, shall we do?   First, we must recognize and accept diversity in biblical interpretation. Equally evangelical students of the Bible read the same texts differently. The diversity presents us an opportunity for fruitful conversation and study in the church. Because we are not dealing with a confessional issue that affects the evangelical theology or churchly identity of the church, we need to bless this honest diversity and free people and churches to come to different conclusions on the basis of careful study and sincere convictions.

Secondly, all the writers in this book agree that we need to affirm all the gifts irrespective of gender. God's Spirit gifts all Christians. Ministry is a function of baptism into the church. Baptism by water and the Spirit affects a gifting by God. All the gifts are to be enabled for ministry.

We agree with James Packer, evangelical theologian of Regent College. The church must give theological priority to gifts over offices in structuring the ministry of the church. The gifts are God's gifts to the church, not ours. All the gifts should be recognized, enabled and exercised for the well-being of the church. These gifts include leaders whose responsibility is to order and enable the many diverse gifts for the effective functioning of the whole. Church offices or church governance structures are not divinely mandated. Different cultural patterns and congregational preferences are responsible for the institutionalization of gifts into offices. Therefore, the difference in structure between the Jerusalem churches, the Antioch churches, and the Pauline churches. We believe the priority of gifts over office, and then the discernment and enablement of gifts, should be the starting point for all reflections on women and men in church ministry today.

Thirdly, we should use inclusive people language in the church. Why? Because the meaning of words has changed. When our grandparents said that God calls all men to serve the kingdom and the church, they were understood to mean that all Christians, men and women, are called by God to service. If we use the same words today, we are understood to say that God calls men, but not women.

The meaning of words like "man" and "men" has changed because the times have changed. Our grandparents lived in an era when neither women nor men as a whole were conscious that women's experiences were different than men's. Gradually, however, some words became more restricted in meaning. Under the impact of modern scientific and historical thought, some words lost the ability to have generic meaning and took on specific meaning. "Men" no longer denoted all people, but men as males in contrast to women as females. Women became conscious of themselves as female. As this consciousness grew, language changed even further.

Our grandparents used inclusive language, but now the same words are considered exclusive. They shut out over half the members of the church, and may act as a hindrance to the mission of the church as it seeks to reach unbelieving men and women. We need to learn to use inclusive language in the church, language that recognizes and blesses all people in their maleness and femaleness.

Fourthly, we must deal honestly and compassionately with contemporary fear and anxiety about changing role identities. We do not believe that the real issues concerning women in church ministry are biblical, but psychological and sociological. The deeper issues are personal questions of sexuality, power and personal identity. These changes are even more complicated because we have based traditional self-understandings and roles on our understanding of what the Bible teaches.

Men have been in power for centuries; they have been able to control the powerless—women—and to exhort them to be submissive and content. They have been conditioned to view women as sexual objects, temptations and distractions. Too often they have held women responsible for their [men's] sins, especially sexual sins. When all of that changes, when men are asked, even forced by the larger pressures in the culture, to accept and respect women as equals and as colleagues, male identity is threatened at its profoundest levels. It is time for the church to talk openly and honestly about male anxieties in times of massive cultural and personal change. Such honest and compassionate conversation in the church will also help address one of the profoundest indices of this fear and insecurity, male abuse of women in the home and in the church.

Women are also afraid. With increasing freedom comes the responsibility of choice. Many women are threatened by the changing demands of the culture. They are afraid that the roles of homemaker and mother will be devalued. They do not always understand the desire of some women to exercise leadership gifts in the church. Again, honest and compassionate conversation is needed to bring about acceptance of the diversity of gifts to be found in the church.

We conclude with a note from church history. There is an almost total disappearance of arguments about gender roles in the church during times of spiritual renewal. Revival-based equality stands in contrast to much current concern in the church with figuring out a "correct" view of women in ministry. Kari Malcolm, a Wheaton College graduate, says it well: "We have a world to win for Christ. The ship is sinking, we are standing on the shore arguing about who should go to the rescue—men or women" (Malcolm, 132).

ENDNOTES

Daly, Mary. The Church and the Second Sex. Harper, 1975.

Foh, Susan T. Women and the Word of God: A Response to Biblical Feminism. Baker, reprint, 1980.

Gasque, Ward and Laurel. "F.F. Bruce: A Mind for What Matters." Christianity Today (April 7, 1989): 22-25.

Malcolm, Kari. Women at the Crossroads. InterVarsity, 1982.

Packer, J. I. "Understanding the Differences." Women, Authority and the Bible, ed. Alvera Michelsen. InterVarsity, 1986. 295-99.

Redekop, Gloria Neufeld. "The Understanding of Woman's Place among Mennonite Brethren in Canada: A Question of Biblical Interpretation". Conrad Grebel Review 8 (1990): 259-274.

Scholer, David M. "Feminist Hermeneutics and Evangelical Biblical Interpretation." Journal of the Evangelical Theological Society 30 (1987): 407-420.

ABOUT THE AUTHORS

Raymond O. Bystrom is Assistant Professor of Pastoral Ministries at Mennonite Brethren Biblical Seminary in Fresno, California. He has served two pastorates in British Columbia, Killarney Park in Vancouver, and Cedar Park in Delta.

David Ewert is Visiting Professor of New Testament at Mennonite Brethren Biblical Seminary. He is a leading New Testament teacher among the Mennonite Brethren, having taught at Mennonite Brethren Bible College in Winnipeg, Manitoba, Mennonite Brethren Biblical Seminary in Fresno, and Eastern Mennonite Seminary in Harrisonburg, Virginia.

Timothy Geddert is on a three-year service leave (1990-93) as Assistant Professor of New Testament at Mennonite Brethren Biblical Seminary. He and his wife, Gertrud, are serving as pastoral couple in Ingolstad, Germany. Tim previously served as pastor in Fort McMurray, Alberta.

Allen R. Guenther is Professor of Old Testament at Mennonite Brethren Biblical Seminary. He has served as a pastor in Alberta and Ontario, and as an instructor at Mennonite Brethren Bible College in Winnipeg, Manitoba.

Edmund Janzen is moderator of the Mennonite Brethren Churches in North America, and professor of biblical studies at Fresno Pacific College in Fresno, California. He has served as a pastor in North Dakota and California.

Elmer A. Martens is Professor of Old Testament at Mennonite Brethren Biblical Seminary. He has served as a pastor in California, and as President of the Seminary.

Gordon H. Matties is a professor of Old Testament at Mennonite Brethren Bible College in Winnipeg, Manitoba.

Lorraine E. Matties is a homemaker and free-lance writer in Winnipeg, Manitoba.

Marilyn Peters is a homemaker and business woman in Fresno, California. She is a graduate of Mennonite Brethren Biblical Seminary and has done advanced studies in church history.

Katrina Poetker is a doctoral student in New Testament at Emory University in Atlanta, Georgia. She and her husband, Alden, have recently completed a missionary assignment in Sao Paulo, Brazil, under Mennonite Brethren Missions/Services.

Valerie Rempel is Administrative Assistant to the Academic Dean and Director of Admissions at Mennonite Brethren Biblical Seminary. She is completing an M.A. in church history.

John E. Toews is Academic Dean and Professor of New Testament at Mennonite Brethren Biblical Seminary. He also has taught at Fresno Pacific College in Fresno, Conrad Grebel College in Waterloo, Ontario, and Tabor College in Hillsboro, Kansas.

Katie Funk Wiebe is Professor Emeritus of Tabor College, Hillsboro, Kansas. She taught English at Tabor for 23 years, and is the author of ten books and hundreds of articles.

DISCUSSION QUESTIONS

Chapter 1

1. The Mennonite Brethren Church began as a movement among like-minded people who wanted to be biblical in a churchly reading of the Bible. Members of the church met to study the Bible and ask, "What does the Bible say?" What is the role of the local congregation today in becoming an "interpreting" community with regard to issues that affect its life together? How should Mennonite Brethren determine which interpretation to use when Bible teachers hold to various interpretations?

2. The topic of women's ministry has two sides, as John E. Toews explains. Clarify what these two sides are. Have class members share their experiences with both sides of the issue.

3. What factors in our society and in our churches have brought the issue of women's ministry to a head? Consider such factors as biblical scholarship, emphasis on gifts, women's education, smaller families, careers and jobs for women, the professionalization of traditional women's ministries, such as health care and hospitality.

4. You will frequently come across the term "restrictive texts" in this book. They are primarily 1 Corinthians 11:2-16, 14:34-36, and 1 Timothy 2:11-15. Read these over in several versions before you begin this study.

Chapter 2

1. Have the class list examples of women, living or dead, whom they think of as having a spiritual ministry. List the various types of ministries included in this list. How does it differ from men's ministries?

2. It is often said that God will only call women to leadership positions if no able men are available. Was this true for Miriam, Huldah, Deborah, Esther, Ruth, Lydia, and Phoebe?

3. In what sense was God's covenant with the Israelites intended for both women and men? How was Sarah included in the covenant?

Chapter 3

1. What does it mean for men and women, single as well as married, to be made in the image of God? How does this affect our understanding of God? Of ourselves? Of our responsibilities as citizens of this planet?

2. Why did God create two sexes? Consider reasons such as procreation and companionship. Can you think of others?

3. A key issue for discussion in Chapters 2, 3, and 4 is whether the pronouncement of the curse on Adam and Eve is a prescription for the roles of men and women as the will of God for all time or a description of the outcome of humanity's sin, which Christ came to redeem. How do you resolve it?

4. African-Americans were kept in submission during slavery because some people saw this arrangement as "natural," or a God-given order. Can this historical event be used to argue for women's equality by analogy?

Chapter 4

1. You will find alternative interpretations of the word "helper" in succeeding chapters. Be sure you understand what they are. If "helper" means the woman is equal to but expected to submit to her husband as leader of the home, what implications does this have for marriage? If "helper" means one who is equal to and mutually shares in family decision-making, what implications does this have for marriage? For male/female relationships in a congregation? Withhold final judgment until you have studied Chapters 9 and 10.

2. How did the Fall alter the relationship of man and woman together, and both to God? Do the judgments pronounced on man and woman, following the break in their relationship to each other and to God, intend to establish the situation for all time, or do they indicate that God's intention was a restoration of the pre-Fall relationships?

3. Since varying positions exist within our denominational membership and all appeal to the Scriptures in support of their views, how can value judgments be avoided while acknowledging sexual differences?

4. Review the questions in Chapter 3 in light of what Chapter 4 teaches.

Chapter 5

1. Proverbs 31 is a poem in praise of a character type. List the kinds of activities the woman was involved in both inside and outside the home.

2. In what ways were women honored, respected, and protected in Old Testament times? What limitations were placed upon them?

3. The writers of this chapter state that the example of the male priesthood in Israel cannot be used to argue the exclusion of women from leadership in the church. Review their arguments. How do you respond to them?

4. How do you envision Joel's words about women "prophesying" in the last days coming to pass (Joel 2:28-29)?

5. How does our knowledge of God's vision for humanity enable us to interpret the specific situations regarding women's role and ministry in the Old Testament?

Chapter 6

1. What are the main characteristics of a good friendship? Do you see these qualities present in Jesus' relationship with Mary and Martha?

2. Mary was the first person to meet the resurrected Christ and the first to receive a message "to go tell." Why did the angel and then Jesus entrust women with this important message first? The question has several aspects. Some scholars say it was because they were doing their womanly duty to prepare dead bodies. Other say it was because they were faithful. Discuss.

3. From the gospel accounts, how do we know that women were part of Jesus' audiences?

4. List examples from the gospels of Jesus' radical relationship to the women of his time. Why didn't he include women among the twelve disciples?

5. Can you think of a woman Jesus criticized? How do you explain what you find or do not find?

6. How does Jesus' attitude toward and relationship with women guide our understanding of the issue?

Chapter 7

1. Read Romans 16 and Philippians 4. Then list the names of women and their ministry. Do you see a pattern evolving?

2. How should a true son or daughter of Abraham be recognized (Luke 3:8; 19:8-9)?

3. Is the issue of women's rights and slavery (civil rights) related to Galatians 3:28? Why didn't Paul speak more directly to issues of racial and sexual prejudice?

4. How would you summarize Paul's practice regarding the ministry of women?

Chapter 8

1. Over the years the church has changed its thinking about the wearing of a headcovering. In an earlier period some women quickly threw an apron or cloth over their heads to observe this custom at family prayers. Why has this custom been dropped?

2. Compare the view of "head" as source with the view in Chapter 3.

3. How do you reconcile the teaching of women's submission to men (with the implication of maintenance of headship, or power) with the teaching of the servanthood of all, which entails giving up power and sacrificing for one another?

4. Is there an advantage for both men and women to remain single if they want to serve the Lord fully?

5. What is your understanding of the church as a "chosen people, a royal priesthood, a holy nation, a people belonging to God"? How important is this understanding of the church as a priesthood to the discussion of the use of men's and women's gifts?

6. What is the difference between status and function (role)? Do their meanings overlap? Can men and women have equal status but different functions within the church?

7. Can biblical teachings be interpreted faithfully apart from a knowledge of the particular historical and cultural situation in which they were written and the audience to which they were addressed?

Chapter 9

1. What responsibilities do Christian families have to oppose social and cultural patterns that are contrary to the teaching of Scripture regarding the home and family life?

2. What does it mean for a husband to love his wife, "just as Christ loved the church and gave himself up for her"? Does the Bible command women to obey their husbands or is this their choice?

3. Much recent research indicates that wife and child abuse is more frequent in homes where husbands believe in a narrow interpretation of women's submission. Why might this be the case?

4. Examine carefully the idea that only equals can submit to one another. Consider the Old Testament bondservant who pledged lifelong servitude only after he was a free man.

5. If single men and women (widowed, never-married, divorced) are not included in Paul's admonitions to husbands and wives, what is their status and function in the church?

Chapter 10

1. Outline the three different interpretations of 1 Timothy 2:11-15. Which do your prefer? Why?

2. What are ways that some Christian women manipulate husbands to get their own way?

3. If the Timothy passage refers to the family situation and not to the congregation, what changes will that make in your thinking?

Chapter 11

1. Why do new and reform movements tend to be open to the ministry of women whereas the institutionalized church is often restrictive?

2. How can we recognize outbursts of Spirit-directed activity, or breakthroughs of a sovereign God in the church? Is it possible that the Spirit may be doing a new thing, but that we may not recognize it as God's working?

3. How are gifts of members in your congregation discerned, called forth and utilized? Who in your congregation is responsible for the calling forth of gifts of all members?

Chapter 12

1. How can we emphasize the common ground men and women share in the ministry of the church and avoid adversarial roles?

2. What kinds of encouragement does your congregation give to both young women and men to enter Christian service?

3. What careers for girls and women are portrayed in our church periodicals and curriculum materials? Is the range of options adequate? Too narrow?

4. What Mennonite Brethren women do you hold up as role models or mentors for your daughters and friends? Read the stories of a number of courageous women of faith in Women Among the Brethren edited by Katie Funk Wiebe.

5. Have someone research the difference between ordination and commissioning and report to the class.

Chapter 13

1. How can we avoid the battle of prooftexting in a discussion of a topic such as this, which has various interpretations, all with biblical support? Can all parts of Scripture actually be harmonized? Consider some other controversial issues like the mode of baptism. Will we always be faced with some passages we cannot fully understand? Should this concern us?

2. Discuss the two main interpretations of the biblical passages dealing with creation order as they relate to the roles of women. What are the points of agreement? of disagreement?

3. Why is it possible for people equally committed to the inspiration and authority of the Bible to disagree on the interpretation of certain passages?

4. How do we move the dialogue from a small group to the entire congregation? How can we remain in dialogue with the Bible about this matter and other culturally-related issues?

5. How much should we consider the value of experience in our discussion? Men want to work at theology, but women will frequently argue from experience.

6. Do we need to think of the Bible in new ways? Instead of thinking of the Scriptures only as what God did in the past, is it important to think of what God is continuing to do and still plans to do, as during the Reformation period, for example?

7. Where is the wind of the Holy Spirit blowing in our churches today? We are often unaware how much we are driven by the spirit of our times. Where is God doing a new thing in our midst and expanding the walls of our tent?

8. Why is the question of women in ministry an issue in our culture?

9. This chapter closes with the question: "What shall we do in the church?" What is your response to this question?